HOW TO FRANCHISING SUCCEED IN

MARK LAUGHLIN

HOW TO SUCCEED IN FRANCHISING

ISBN 978-1-61961-339-3

LIONCREST
PUBLISHING

To Graham MacLean, my grandfather who taught me how to listen.

CONTENTS

FOREWORD

As a 45-year veteran of the franchise industry, I am often asked two particular questions from potential franchise buyers more than any other questions: one, *"what is the right way to investigate a franchise industry opportunity?"* and two, *"why do they need a consultant to help them in this investigation?"*

My answers might seem simple and obvious, but I cannot stress the importance of these considerations:

First, START WITH ASSUMING you need to know the basics of franchising—because it operates *differently* and *under a different set of business laws* than corporate America or privately-owned business. In other words, even if you come from a sophisticated business background, you may have a lot more to learn than you think.

The franchise industry has over 3,000 companies across

approximately twenty different industries. Like any major industry, the franchise industry has many very good companies that offer spectacular opportunities in which to invest, but it also has some rotten apples as well, or even well-known companies that have seen better days. I might say that it's not that terribly different from the stock market in that regard.

Being on the outside of the franchise industry, looking in, the average person does not know a good franchise investment from a bad one, or frankly even the right questions to ask in an investigative process—again, *even those coming from fairly broad business backgrounds.* Because the *same rules don't apply* as do those you may use for reviewing an established business or a stock. In franchising, and ONLY in franchising, one has to take FAR more than potential financial returns into consideration—or your "love" or interest for the product—*because a good franchise is only as good as its owner.* Without the right "match" of the franchise model—to your passions, your skill sets, AND your lifestyle and financial goals—unfortunate mistakes in investment can be made. I'd go even further to say that most individuals that I have spoken to or helped through the years began their investigation process ONLY "thinking like consumers," and looking for companies in which they found the "product offered for sale" to be of interest. A BIG MISTAKE!

A highly-trained franchise consultant can assist a potential buyer "delve into" this industry—not only by introducing them to the better, *pre-screened* companies, but in helping them assess their skill sets, their passions, their lifestyle, and their financial needs—but will also provide them with valuable education about how a "good a franchise works with its owners." In other words, they guide prospects to the "short list" that will be appropriate for what they truly need and want for their family's financial future.

Now, HOW DO YOU FIND A REALLY GOOD CONSULTANT?

I explain that a top-tier consultant must have some very serious credentials. He should have been a senior level executive with several different companies in the industry. He should have been in the franchise industry for at least 20 years. He should have owned one or more franchises/businesses himself, and he should be able to demonstrate to you his knowledge of this industry *well beyond* simply telling you the name of companies in which he was employed.

Furthermore, a really good consultant will not only have helped hundreds of people find the right business, but more importantly will also tell many others not to invest—when their personal skill sets or goals or financial status do not blend well with requirements for being a successful business owner.

In MARK LAUGHLIN, you have found such an executive franchise consultant. Having been in the industry over 30 years, as well as having owned a number of very successful businesses, Mark has *been there, done that.*

He has assisted hundreds of people find the right businesses. And, as I mentioned earlier, being the man of ethics that he is, he has also counseled many, many people *not to buy* a franchise.

Mark has been our consulting group's *Franchise Consultant of the Year* for the last two years in a row, and I can truly tell you that he is not only considered **one of the best in the industry** by us, but by the hundreds of franchise company executives with whom he interacts every day.

In Mark Laughlin, you have found the professional that you need—to help you meet your goals and achieve your business ownership aspirations.

Chris Wright
President & CEO
The YOU Network
www.theyounetwork.com

INTRODUCTION

Meet Steve.

It's early 2013, and he's just lost his longstanding position with a New Jersey packaging company. After several months of fruitless job searching, he decides to take matters into his own hands. He decides to take a look at franchising.

That's when he and I crossed paths.

With my guidance, we looked at a number of different franchise brands, and then Steve whittled that list down to a small handful. Steve did his research, vetting them out, and then made his decision. It was probably the best professional decision of his life. He signed on with Electronic Restoration Services (ERS).

Based in Ann Arbor, Michigan, ERS is a repair service that

handles any type of electronic item damaged by fire or flood. They don't work with the end consumer; they work with either insurance companies or with disaster restoration companies like Servpro or ServiceMaster. Their service is truly a win-win: The insurance companies win because, much of the time, these items simply need to be cleaned—not replaced—so they save a great deal of money, and franchisees such as Steve win because the profit margins are excellent.

FOLLOWING THE BLUEPRINT

Steve has gone on to achieve great success. How? One of the key factors is that he got himself into a niche business. It's basically recession-proof; accidents are going to happen regardless of the economy and repairs will be needed.

The other thing that he did right was follow the blueprint the franchisor gave him. This is absolutely critical. Per the ERS franchisee blueprint, in the first couple of months, he hit the road and introduced himself to all the disaster restoration companies in his regions. He followed the ERS model to a T—many franchisees don't—and he continues to do so 18 months later.

One of the unique value propositions (UVP) about this particular franchisor was the size of its territories. Each one is very large with about two million people. His state, New Jersey, is broken into four territories. He was awarded two territories, opened up his business and established a positive cash flow very quickly. Before long, he purchased a third territory in N.J. Fast forward to January 2015: Steve bought a fourth ERS territory in Pennsylvania, and a fifth territory in Staten Island and a sixth territory that encompasses part of Manhattan. Steve's ERS now services a territory of 10 million people in three states.

Beyond his success as a franchisee, Steve has established what we call a "legacy business", which down the road he might turn over to one of his kids. If we were to choose a perfectly executed franchise plan, Steve would be the poster boy.

A HISTORY OF SUCCESS

According to some accounts, the concept of franchising goes back to the Middle Ages, when a king would grant distribution rights to the brewmaster, who made the best beer in the region. The king endorsed the beer and was given a "royalty" or a percentage of the brewmaster's business.

In America, the concept goes back more than a century. Back in the 1880s, the idea was similar to our contemporary model of franchising. Franchisees would pay a franchisor for the rights to sell a particular product. Each party would benefit: the franchisees would be representing a known quantity, while the franchisor would receive a guaranteed stream of income in the form of franchising fees.

It's important to note that, in order to succeed, both sides had to pull their weight back then. The franchisee had to be adept at selling or at managing his sales team, and the franchisor needed to provide quality products.

So it is today. As a franchisee, you have the opportunity to represent a product or service without the hassle of starting from scratch. Although the franchisor will provide much in the way of logistical support, it's really up to you, the franchisee, to put all your weight into selling the product or providing the service. It truly is a rewarding arrangement if you meet the criteria in terms of your financial resources, professional talents and personality. And that's what this book is about.

If you have the drive and desire to open a franchise, then I suggest you follow the advice found in the pages that follow. While I cannot guarantee your success, you will be armed with enough information to begin to make the right decisions for you and your family.

AVOIDING COMMON PITFALLS

At some point in their lives, most people think about going into business for themselves; franchises can provide that unique opportunity. But there's more to being successful than being offered the opportunity to become a franchisee with Super Cuts—a lot more.

One factor to consider is motivation. A big mistake I see people make is going into the wrong business for the wrong reason. Why does this happen? Because they don't evaluate themselves. For example, some people will jump in to a sales-driven model when they have no sales skills. In many cases, a good franchisor will vet that out with a service such as Franchise Navigator (More on that later in the book).

Self-evaluation is crucial. If I have a client who's an engineer, an architect or an accountant who does not have a whole lot of personality, as a franchise consultant, I'm very limited to what I can show them because in most cases (a) they can't sell; (b) they're not going to network; and (c) they probably can't run a small team of people.

Other big mistakes:

- People choose a franchise because it's cheap. They base their decision on the entry price into the business.
- They base their decision on what one or two owners are making in a particular franchise.
- They don't know how to research properly and don't know how to vet a company.

THE 98 PERCENT

Many people, at some point in their life, consider starting their own business. The reality is maybe 2 percent of them will actually do so in their lifetime. What about the remainder? What's holding them back? There are three main reasons.

One reason is fear. Take somebody that's been collecting a steady paycheck and benefits his or her entire life. Start a franchise business and that security blanket is gone during ramp up time.

I've acted as a franchise consultant for numerous clients and every single one has experienced different levels of nervousness and anxiety. It's natural. Fear, doubt and doom are always playing a concert on your front porch. Some people get scared after their original conversation with me and don't go any further. Some get scared when it becomes time to investigate franchise brands. Some get scared when it's time to talk to franchisors. And some folks are looking for any reason not to do business.

On the initial consultation, I tell my clients that we all go through moments of self-doubt. As a matter of fact, I get nervous when somebody *doesn't* have a little bit of fear. There's potential danger in being a little bit too sure of yourself when making such a huge decision.

Reason number two that causes a person to avoid starting a business is something I call the "spousal ambush." How does your "better half" or significant other feel about your newfound entrepreneurial spirit? It's a question that I ask very early in the process. If your spouse is not onboard, you will not be getting into business—plain and simple.

From my side of the desk, spousal ambush is a no-win situation. I certainly don't want to cause a divorce, so I extricate myself from the situation pretty quickly unless I can get the spouse to engage in the investigation process. And if your spouse isn't onboard with your business idea, you too should head for the exit.

The third problematic reason: relying on the opinion of an uninformed, but well-intentioned third party. In all likelihood, you have a circle of influence—a network of family members, friends and neighbors—from whom you might be tempted to solicit advice. Beware! Their responses, while goodhearted, are often based on ignorance or on anecdotal experiences.

For example, you run over to a neighbor's house and announce that you're thinking of purchasing a residential cleaning franchise. Your neighbor's comment: "Why would you need a franchise for that business?" Or this: "Jack in the Box? Didn't they have all that trouble a few years ago?"

What do remarks like these have to do with these businesses in the here and now? What purpose do remarks like these serve, other than to (unintentionally) rain on your parade?

Turning your dream business into reality should be done purposefully, with great care. Remember, it's a brave step with some potential pitfalls. But you—and only you—can become the entrepreneur extraordinaire you want to be.

A COMPLEX PLAYING FIELD

There are approximately 3,000 franchises in more than 70 categories spread out across the USA. Navigating that playing field can be confusing, which is why you need this book. It will show you how to run your own business by leveraging the power of franchises.

That power is considerable. If you were to open up your own business, chances are you would not have a marketing person, an IT person or an operations person reporting to you. With a franchise, you have access to all of these personnel. When you join a franchise, you'll be able to leverage proven systems and processes; branding; specialized technology; access to staff; and expertise that you wouldn't be able to afford on your own. If you don't see the true value you're getting for your ongoing fees, then franchising isn't for you.

With a franchise, you'll know how you're progressing and you'll see if your sales numbers aren't where they're supposed to be. Your franchisor should sit down with you and tell you how you're doing compared to others that opened up in the same time frame, in your region, and how you're doing on a national basis. You'll see if your payroll or cost of goods is too high, and if your average ticket is in line with others in the system.

Doing such calculations can be onerous if you're doing them on your own, but many franchisors have proprietary software that can save you an incredible amount of time.

This book also intends to clarify popular misconceptions. For example, when most people think about franchises, they think of Subway or McDonalds, but fast food franchises are just the beginning. They aren't a good fit for many people because many of the fast food premium brands are out of the average person's price range. Most folks don't have the net worth and liquid capital requirements to open a Panera Bread or a Dunkin Donuts.

As you'll see in this book, alternatives abound. We'll touch on many other franchise categories, from automotive shops and hair cutting salons to workout facilities. And that's just skimming the surface.

As I mentioned earlier, franchising is complicated and most people have no idea where to start. Many will end up being taken advantage of or become confused, and some will fail. This book is designed to save you all that stress and teach you the most important things you'll need to succeed.

LET ME INTRODUCE MYSELF

My name is Mark Laughlin. I've spent many years helping future business owners find the right franchise and go through the sometimes-daunting process of setting things up.

My roots in the franchising industry are deep. My wife and I owned a Postal Instant Press for nine years. We also owned a Molly Maid franchise and an Inches-A-Weigh workout facility, which was a diet and workout place for women. For several years, I worked on the other side of the fence as a Franchise Development Coordinator for Spectrum Home Services and Fibrenew USA.

As someone with many years experience in the franchising industry, I've seen people make all kinds of mistakes. I saw them make mistakes when I was a franchisee; I saw them make mistakes when I worked on the franchisor side; and now, when I see people making mistakes, I try to correct them in my role as a franchise coach.

To date, I've helped more than 250 people get into business. Consider this book a private consultation, designed to get you on your feet as a franchisee. I want you to have a great experience. Above all, I want you to find the right company with the right territory.

IT'S ALL ABOUT YOU

This book has been written for anybody who is in a dead-end job; anybody that feels that they're going to be pink-slipped or become a victim of downsizing; or anybody who has already lost their job. It's also for someone interested in building equity in themselves. When you work for somebody, you get a paycheck at the end of the day and perhaps some benefits. That's it. Period.

Franchise businesses, on the other hand, create a whole lot of value. Consider this: At some point in the future, it's going to be time to sell that business. A well-run franchise business will typically sell for a multiplier of EBITDA, or earnings before interest, taxes, depreciation and amortization. Usually two-and-a-half to five times that amount.

This is a benefit unavailable to the typical wage-slave. Your reward for your sweat equity. I call it the pot of gold at the end of the rainbow.

This book is divided into three main parts. In Part One, "Assess Yourself," you'll learn how to evaluate your financial condition as it pertains to purchasing a franchise, plus ways to fund your new business. You'll see how your family situation can impact the success of your franchise, and you'll take a long, hard look at yourself. Do you have the personality traits necessary to be a success in franchising? And given your personality, what type of franchise is the right fit for you?

In Part Two, "Find and Apply," you'll get an overview of how franchises work. You'll learn rock-solid techniques for looking at the right franchises. And in the third part of the book, you will learn the value of completing the Franchisors Pre-Training Checklist before you attend the franchisor's off-site training and how to sidestep common mistakes.

Time to dig in! I'm confident that if you follow the guidance provided in the coming pages, you will be well on your way to taking control of your business destiny and establishing a bright financial future for yourself and your family.

PART ONE

ASSESSING
YOURSELF

———

FINANCIAL ASSESSMENT

A foundation built on solid finances is essential to success with a franchise. In this chapter, we'll examine how much money you need to get started with your franchise, some common monetary mistakes and various ways to finance your business.

MONETARY REQUIREMENTS

It's a simple fact of life: You're going to have to come up with some cash. You see, every franchisor has their own financial requirements for their potential franchisees, including a net worth requirement and a liquid capital requirement. How much is required?

Category #1

On the high end of the spectrum, a franchisor requires several million in net worth and liquid around $150k - $600k. Many retail outlets fall into this category:

- Fast-food franchises
- Hair salons with the larger chains
- Automotive maintenance/repair shops
- Massage/spa services

Category #2

On the lower end of the spectrum, a franchisor requires about $250,000 net worth and $50,000–$75k liquid. Falling into this category would be the majority of service models that include:

- Handyman franchises
- Cleaning franchises
- Disaster-restoration franchises
- Sales-oriented franchises where the one employee might be you, or a business that doesn't require retail space and have huge expenses.

The vast majority falls into one of these two categories. You probably won't be surprised when I tell you that these requirements eliminate many people.

Some people are still reeling from the real estate crisis; their houses are still underwater. Some have accumulated large credit card debts with big monthly payments. Many may have kids in college with loans. Short version: Things aren't going financially well for these families. Whatever the reason, these people simply cannot afford to apply for a franchise.

REALITY CHECK

A crucial part of your financial assessment is adding up your monthly household expenses. You'll need to answer this question: How much do you need to run your household?

If you have a spouse who's working, that's a big bonus because it will take away a lot of pressure. *It's key to remember that franchise businesses do not make money overnight.*

So how long does it take before you're making money? With a service business, you might achieve a positive cash flow in six to eight months. I was always able to achieve that myself. But in a retail business in which you're paying rent, it could take several years. So you must be able to put down the initial fees upfront and then, separately, make certain that you have your living expenses covered.

At my company, we occasionally meet people with absolutely unrealistic expectations. I spoke to a guy who told me that he's pulling down $200,000 a year. His request: "Find me something where I can replace that income in the first year." I told him I can't. They don't exist.

I recently took a call from a person in New York who told me that he needed to make $2,000,000 a year. "I don't want to work very hard," he said, "and I've got $100,000 to invest."

As you can imagine, that was a pretty short conversation.

TAPPING INTO YOUR 401(K)

A very common way to finance your franchise is through a 401(k) rollover. It just makes sense for some people to utilize funds that are at their disposal. There is a significant advantage to doing this; one that most people are unaware of.

Most people don't know they can rollover their 401(k) and use it to start a business *without paying any prepayment penalties or federal taxes*. When I say, "most people don't know", this (surprisingly) includes many clueless accountants and financial planners. This arrangement is part of the ROBS program: Rollovers as Business Start-ups. Recently, I had a phone discussion with FranFund's CEO, Geoff Seiber, in which we talked about the ROBS program and how it might help you in funding your franchise. Here's what he had to say:

Mark: Can you go through some of the basics of the program?

Geoff: With the Rollover for Business Start-Ups (ROBS) program, clients are able to utilize their qualified retirement funds to capitalize their business tax- and penalty-free. Retirement plan rollovers are a very popular funding strategy for purchasing a new business and can be used as the equity injection for a loan or as the entire investment.

With a FranPlan (FranFund's 401(k) Rollover product), the client is basically investing their retirement funds into their own company stock. The process begins when FranFund helps the client form a new corporation, which then sponsors a 401(k) plan. Funds are rolled from the client's current 401(k) or IRA to the new 401(k) plan, which then purchases shares in the newly formed corporation. The corporation will now be able to use the retirement funds to purchase the client's new business or franchise.

Mark: Can you talk about using retirement funds you haven't paid taxes on to fund your project?

Geoff: Utilizing these funds to capitalize their business allows the client to invest in themselves. They are in control of the growth, profitability and ultimate success of their retirement investment. By avoiding unnecessary taxes and penalties, the client has access to more of their funds and is able to save more money for retirement.

The IRS has determined that these 401(k) funds are an acceptable source for the cash injection required for SBA loans. In addition, these funds are a great way to supplement other funding vehicles to enable the client to purchase a larger or multi-unit business or franchise.

Mark: How long does this process take?

Geoff: The average time it takes to fully fund a client is less than 15 business days. Clients that take advantage of FranFund's Safety Net Program can shorten that timeframe to as little as five business days. The two biggest variables that impact this timing are client motivation and response, and how long it takes for the current custodian to send the funds to Merrill Lynch. Each custodian and plan has a different process for rolling over assets, which can vary the time it takes for the client to be funded.

Mark: Describe your Safety Net program.

Geoff: The FranPlan (401(k) rollover) process normally takes

15 to 20 business days, with the longest portion of that time being the movement of funds from the current custodian to Merrill Lynch.

Utilizing the Safety Net program starts that money movement at no cost to the client. When the money arrives at Merrill Lynch, it is placed in a Conduit IRA until further instruction. Once the client decides to move forward with their business and engage FranFund for the FranPlan, their funds are then available to capitalize their new business in less than five business days.

If the client's plans change and they decide not to move forward with a business, there is nothing to undo, no refunds to collect and their money is safe in a Traditional IRA at Merrill Lynch.

Mark: What about upfront fees and the monthly ongoing fees?

Geoff: The total initial cost for creating a FranPlan is $4,795. The IRS requires that the client utilize a Third Party Administrator (TPA) to manage their plan and to provide the proper checks and balances. This plan administration includes a number of important activities such as completing the forms for the annual 5500 tax filings, updating the plan with all IRS-required plan amendments, testing of 401(k) and matching contributions if applicable, etc. The cost for FranFund to provide this service is $1,320 per year, or $110 monthly. TPA service should begin in the first month after the plan is installed.

Mark: Do you take care of the Incorporation/FEIN Number?

Geoff: Yes. FranFund provides several services associated with the installation of a FranPlan:

- Creates Operating Entity – We prepare and file Articles of Incorporation with appropriate state agency.
- (F)EIN Numbers – We obtain Federal Employer Identification Numbers for the client's corporate and 401(k) plans.
- New Corporate Binder – We prepare corporate organizational documents including Bylaws, Minutes and Initial Stock Certificates.
- New 401(k) Profit Sharing Plan – We prepare 401(k) plan documents including the Plan Document, Trust Agreement and related Plan administration forms.
- Continuous Support – We provide guidance during the entire process, including facilitating the movement of funds from the client's current custodian.
- Third Party Administration – We communicate procedures and requirements for ongoing 401(k) TPA services.

Mark: Can you talk about taking care of IRS filings and business evaluation at the end of the year?

Geoff: FranFund will assist in the process of valuing the company annually as required by the Plan Document and for reporting the value of the company's stock on the Form 5500.

Mark: How does Fran Fund pay the "bump fees" to shorten the registration times in the states that are backed up?

Geoff: FranFund typically pays expediting fees in states where such payments will make the total process go quicker. We try not to let state back-ups interfere with our timelines if possible.

Mark: Why are so many CPAs and financial planners in the dark on how this program works?

Geoff: ERISA law is a very specific part of the Internal Revenue Code (IRC) and even qualified, experienced accountants may not be familiar with this part of the IRC. Over recent years, we have found that more accountants and financial advisors have had some exposure to the ROBS program, but many still have questions as to how this funding strategy will affect what they do for our mutual client. We are always happy to have conversations with a client's accountant and financial advisor to explain how the process works and answer any concerns.

Mark: What happens if I have Roth accounts?

Geoff: In Roth retirement plans, taxes have already been paid on the assets held in the plan. This means that they cannot be rolled into a pre-tax retirement plan, like a 401(k). Since this is not considered a "qualified" plan, it cannot be used in this process.

When considering all sources of funding, Roth money can be put into the business, but the client would have to take distributions from the Roth account, which would be subject to the 10 percent early withdraw penalty if they're under 59

½ years old. In this method, the client would invest or loan this money to the company as if it came from any personal source.

Mark: What types of IRA/401k rollovers are not eligible to participate in this?

Geoff: Any "qualified" retirement plan can be used in the ROBS process. "Qualified" is just another way of saying pre-tax retirement money. Qualified plans include Traditional IRA, 401(k), 403(b), Thrift Savings Plans, Pensions, etc.

Mark: If all of my money is with my current employer, will I have to sever employment and wait for 30 days until my money is available?

Geoff: The client cannot roll money contributed to their current employer's plan without separating from the job first. The process for rolling money from the existing plan will vary depending on the current custodian requirements. We would advise that the employee contact their current plan administrator to get a better idea of the paperwork and timing involved.

Mark: What happens if I am in the middle of a divorce? How long will I have to wait until the money is distributed?

Geoff: It depends. In our experience, most attorneys suggest that the client does not touch retirement plan assets during a divorce. Once the divorce is final, if the court orders that the retirement plan be split between parties, the court will have to sign a separate order called a Qualified Domestic Relations

Order. This will be passed along to the current administrator, who will separate the account. Once the account is separated, the client can roll their account to the 401(k) Plan that FranFund establishes. There are too many factors to address the timing of a situation like this.

Mark: What percentage of people do you not renew every year?

Geoff: We typically range from 3 to 5 percent attrition each year, thus a continuation rate in the high 90 percent range.

If you'd like more information on the ROBS program or on the FranFund, visit www.franfund.com

SBA: USING OTHER PEOPLE'S MONEY

I recently had a conversation with Reg Byrd of Direct Connect Ventures on SBA loans.

Mark: Explain to folks how the SBA process works as far as the SBA guarantying the face value of the loan for the bank. What do they usually guarantee the loan for...90%...80%?

Reg: The SBA guarantees varied percentages of loan amounts that banks lend. For example, the SBA guarantees as much as 85% on loan amounts up to $150,000 and 75% on loans amounts greater than $150,000. The maximum SBA exposure is $3,750,000 therefore one may have an SBA loan (or total of all SBA loans) up to $5,000,000.

Keep in mind that the percentage of SBA guarantee does not correlate with the amount of capital injection (skin-in-the-game) required by a borrower. The guarantee is going to be on whatever the loan amount is regardless of the capital injection. *The two (SBA guarantee and borrower injection) are not to be confused as being the same.*

Mark: Will Congress keep the SBA coffers full in 2016 to encourage folks to open up new businesses?

Reg: In December 2015 President Obama signed the FY16 Omnibus bill. In part, this bill provided the 2-16 SBA budget $26.5 billion for the 7(a) flagship program and $7.5 billion for the 504 program, mainly used for real estate.

Mark: In September of 2015 it looked like they had let that funding run out and then reloaded it?

Reg: The 2015 SBA-backed authorization level for the 7(a) program far exceeded all expectations. The fiscal budget for 2015 had been $18.75 billion and by July it was apparent the $18.75 would be completely allocated with an increase on the horizon. The SBA had begun planning for this early on and by July 28, 2015 the Senate passed legislation that increased the authorization level to $23.5 billion, a $4.75-billion-dollar increase; more than adequate for coverage through the fiscal year (September 31, 2015). The year of 2015 marked the most successful and record breaking years for the SBA.

Mark: How easy or difficult is it for the average person to get an SBA loan?

Reg: The SBA program was founded on July 30, 1953. It had been built with a philosophy and mission to help rebuild Main Street America. This was in response to the pressures of the Great Depression and WWII. Today the original design and purpose of the program remains with its same spirit; to provide lending for those who otherwise wouldn't qualify for traditional bank financing. Granted, it's not "easy" per se to secure an SBA loan; the government is involved! However, knowing exactly how to put a deal together will land the funding.

Mark: Can you get pre-approved like a mortgage on a house?

Reg: Yes, absolutely. In fact, pre-qualification is the only way to go. It's a very efficient and responsible way to begin the journey of securing financing. Regardless of what kind of financing process one goes through (a house, a car, a business) it is going to be arduous! The process should never be started until qualification is in hand. The question one should always ask first is, "Am I bankable?" If so, "What project cost am I qualified for?" The answers to those questions allow control and bring clarity to the process, right out of the gate.

Mark: How long does it usually take to close?

Reg: The financing journey, on average, will take approximately 15 weeks. Keep in mind that during this time other important tasks are getting checked off the to-do list, e.g., site selection, lease negotiations, training, contractor bidding, etc. It's not 15-weeks and then everything else can start. We're talking 15-weeks to grand opening.

Mark: Let's say the total cost of getting into business was a $100k? How much would the bank loan and how much cash infusion would someone need?

Reg: This depends on a number of factors and is difficult to answer specifically. Bear with me. A lender is first going to test the borrower's personal financial composition. The strength of the borrower will play a major role in a lender's decision on how much of the project cost to lend (loan-to-value). If an acquisition (buying an existing business), lenders are more inclined to lend a greater amount. This is because there is historical performance the bank can work from. A startup, on the other hand, is entirely projection based so a lender is going to be more risk averse. When real estate is included as part of the purchase, a lender will have appreciating real property to back the loan. In this case, the debt will be reduced with every payment that's made while the real estate appreciates in value; excellent scenario and so a lender will be open to lender more on the deal.

Generally speaking, as a rule of thumb, a borrower should keep in mind that a startup will require a borrower's injection to be as much as 30% of the total project cost. Beware and stay away from lenders that require 50% injection for *food-related* startups—they're out there! Acquisitions will require anywhere between 15% to 20% injection. Programs including real estate will range from 10% to 20% of the total project cost.

Mark: What else are the banks looking for?

Reg: There are the 5 key criteria lenders are looking for. 1)

Capital available for a) injection into the business and b) personal reserve; 2) Personal outside income to support personal debt service; 3) Credit (and it's not *just* about the score, it's the content being report); 4) Experience in the industry of business being purchased. (Folks—this is not a deal killer is most often only a bank specific requirement!); and 5) Collateral. Like experience, collateral is not a deal killer either! Borrowers who are renters can be just as qualified as someone who owns their own home.

Mark: Equity in a property?

Reg: Equity in real estate is absolutely not a requirement. This is one of the most misunderstood and misrepresented points about financing. As mentioned previously, renters qualify for financing—everyday. There is no lending prejudice regarding one's position with owning real estate, or not. Having equity in property (often times referred to as collateral) can certainly be helpful but does not preclude business lending from being approved. Does it help to have collateral? Sure it does. But... don't stop pursuing just because you don't have any. I even had a lender once tell me that "Collateral is overrated!" His position was to be well informed about one's *entire* financial composition.

Mark: One or both spouses working when they apply?

Reg: One of both spouses working is not a requirement. The requirement is, in fact, that personal outside income (does not mean a "job") must be in place to adequately cover personal annual debt service. In some cases, I've been party to financing being placed for individuals who are not working at all. They might have had an annuity, or trust, that adequately covers their personal annual debt service. Working is not to be confused with outside income. Outside income can be found through different channels.

Mark: Credit scores over 700?

Reg: Don't take this wrong but credit scores are sometimes not the end all. Sure they are always going to be important but credit scores can sometimes be misleading. It's important to analyze why the score is what it is. Delve into what's being reported—that's what is important. For scores less than 670 it's important to understand why. There are credit care facilities that can make a big impact by correcting erroneous or dated information in the credit report.

Mark: How about is someone that has had a short sale or bankruptcy in the past 7 years would that disqualify them from getting an SBA loan?

Reg: As with most negative connotations, a justifiable and legitimate explanation can cure the matter at hand. Let's say a short sale took place because of a required job relocation that came up suddenly. Now, there is a home [underwater] that has to be sold in order to continue employment. If the sale of a home doesn't happen, it would be understood if the home was left behind so that employment would continue. A prospective lender could find this an acceptable reason for the short sale and proceed with underwriting a business loan.

There could very well be a workaround when there's a bankruptcy that was discharged seven years ago. Paramount in the recovery from bankruptcy is the ability to demonstrate an earnest positive effort has been made to rebound since the discharge. Keep in mind there are some lenders that won't touch a borrower request when a bankruptcy is in the past. However, this is simply not the case across the lending board.

Mark: I have worked with many people all over the country. I have only had 4 people in the last 12 years that have been able to get an SBA loan secured locally. Most folks have their application rejected because of incomplete data usually on the marketing plan. What does your company do to make sure this doesn't happen or improve their odds?

Reg: Our Business Plan product is referred to as the "key to the vault." This is because it works, every time. Lenders must adhere to very specific policies regarding business plans that are outlined in SBA procedures manuals. Originally designed around SBA guidelines, our business plan is considered by many lenders as the bar by which all business plans must be received. Years ago I recall a franchisor calling me requesting that I step in with one of his franchisees who was securing lending on their own. The bank had given the franchisee the green light for several months and at the eleventh hour pulled the plug and killed the deal. To make a long story short, ends up I had known the lender for many years. In talking to the lender about why he killed the deal I learned it was because of the lack of detail in the business plan! We took it from there, redid the borrower's business plan they had attempted, had the case re-opened at the bank and the deal was funded.

This isn't the only story of its kind. The business plan will make or break a deal. A lender doesn't want to teach someone how to write a business plan. A lender's position regarding business plans is that if the borrower can't write and compile a business plan, the bank shouldn't lend.

Often we will hear..."Oh, I wrote a couple business plans while in college." "I can write the business plan." Well folks, I'm here to tell you, I wrote business plans in college too but they were nothing like what's required in a *lender's business plan*. Writing a business plan for a business loan is something one might do only once in a lifetime. Leave the writing of a lender's business plan to the ones who write them everyday.

Mark: What do banks accept as collateral on a loan?

Reg: Of course, personal real estate. Lender's will accept just about any kind of an appreciating asset that a borrower has. I've witness lender's using watercraft, fine art, classic vehicles, jewels, etc. Cash too; a CD in the bank can be collateral. If a cash investment (a Certificate of Deposit) was going to stay in the bank anyhow, might as well assign it to the lender to use as collateral. Lender's will also use marketable securities, e.g., stock investment portfolios. Again, if the securities weren't going anywhere, anyhow, might as well allow the bank to use them as collateral. The securities can still be traded for investment purposes, just can't cash them in.

A lender will file a UCC (Uniform Commercial Code) lien on any and all business assets (furniture, fixtures, equipment, etc.). However, business assets often are often already depreciated as they come off the delivery truck—meaning, a lender will only value business assets at sometimes only twenty cents on the dollar, sometimes less.

Keep in mind, though, collateral not required to secure an SBA loan. The SBA procedure a lender must follow is to look for any form of collateral; if collateral exists then the lender must use it. If collateral does not exist, then taking on the program rests with whatever the bank's own policy is. Remember the lender I mentioned who said collateral is over rated? That's a bank with a policy that collateral is not required. Some banks might not require collateral at all, other might require up to 100% of the loan amount, and others 50%. Every lender has their own policy.

Mark: What are the pitfalls in trying to secure an SBA loan right where you live? I find many banks say they do SBA but may only do 2 or 3 a year. I had a situation years ago where a brand new bank employee was processing the paperwork and what should have taken 60-90 days to fund took 8 months.

Reg: Interesting question and comment. After years and years of doing this we have weeded out lenders who cause pitfalls. One pitfall we run into is when the underwriting takes place in a "central" underwriting office and there's no control from our end. When we're unable to communicate with the underwriter directly we will remove the lender from our lender relationship list. We have almost completely eliminated all lenders that have a centralized underwriting center.

Another pitfall is when we have a lender call our customer

directly, without our approval or knowing. If this takes place more than a couple of times, then we will also remove this lender from our relationship list.

At this time, we are well situated with lenders who uphold the same standards of customer respect that we do. The need for constant, mutual communication is critical. Lenders who understand this and share the levels of communication that we do, are those who we will lean on.

Mark: How many loans does your company secure for folks in a year Reg?

Reg: This past year we successfully secured financing for 176 entrepreneurs. The project sized ranged from $75,000 to $4,250,000. There were 382 entrepreneurs whose projects were pre qualified for financing.

Mark: What are the current interest rates at and what are the time lines on the loans?

Reg: There are several SBA lending products that lenders have to chose from. They all have different scales for determining interest rates and these scales are dictated by the SBA. The SBA provides for the "maximum" amount of interest a lender can impose on a borrower and leaves the final decision to the lender.

The maximum rate is made up of two parts: a base rate and a fixed amount. The base rate generally administered is the Wall Street Journal Prime Rate (currently 3.5%).

Our mainstream business is cause for lenders to administer the rules of the most popular SBA product; the 7(a). We are finding most of our programs coming back from lenders in the range of the Prime + 1.75 to 2.75 points. The interest rate for startup projects will almost always be variable, not fixed.

Mark: Is it easier to get an SBA loan in 2016 say on a service business under $125K than it was in 2009-2010?

Reg: Oh my goodness, yes. Just about everything in lending is "easier" now than it was in 2009 and 2010! The approach for financing must always be to know your lenders. Know what the lender's appetite is and don't waste anybody's time going to a lender for a service related business when the lender doesn't even lend for such models. This is when having tight relationships with lenders is golden. You present what the lender's appetite is for, and deals get done.

Another worthwhile note to make here is that lenders are now very confident about what they will and won't take on. The lender's clarity in todays lending environment moves processes along quickly. Lenders know what they want to do, can do and will do. We no longer hear the line..."Well, let's take a look and we'll see." Phew, glad those days are over!

Mark: How important is that the franchisor be on the SBA fast track registry. For the readers would you explain what the fast track registry is?

Reg: It is crucial that a lender be approved by the Franchise Registry (the Registry). The Registry works directly with the

SBA in providing a streamlined process for a franchisor to become SBA approved. In fact, our relationship with the Registry has grown over the years. We need to have franchise systems approved in the Registry. In fact, there are even some of our lenders who have informed us they will no longer lend for franchises systems that are not approved on the Registry!

In some cases, while being approved on the Registry is necessary, there are products the Registry generates that will give a lender the sense of comfort they need about a franchise. Having the tools the Registry provides allows our firm to make a sell to a lender that otherwise the lender might not have taken on. A lender isn't just underwriting a borrower; they are also underwriting the franchise concept. Very soon, scores are going to be given to franchises. Similar to FICO, the Registry is close to launching the *FUND report!* SBA lenders across the nation will soon begin relying on the *FUND report* and the *FUND score* for a franchise to determine if they will lend for a particular franchise concept.

Mark: Do banks look at the failure rate on SBA loans over the past 10 years with a particular franchisor and would that disqualify an individual from getting a loan if that rate was deemed a high %? What would be deemed a high failure rate?

Reg: Unfortunately, there are still some lenders who rely on a failure rate to determine if they will lend, or not. It has been publicly announced by the SBA that figures being used by independent consulting companies who generate a Failure Report are completely inaccurate. For years the SBA has been miscoding statistical data into their database. These miscodes have caused the reporting of failure data on franchises that is entirely inaccurate.

For example: 'Hair Salon A' franchise had an SBA loan default. The SBA input the default into the database of 'Hair Salon B'. Oops! Now Hair Salon B is showing a failure not belonging to them, but instead belongs to Hair Salon A!

The Registry is working daily to scrub the SBA's database and to "restate" failure rates. Lenders wise of the erroneous data will often request a Bank Credit Report ("BCR") from a franchise. The BCR is where lenders can find the restated failure data along with a detailed report of unit and franchise system performance.

To that end, a franchise approved on the Registry is virtually a requirement in today's lending environment.

Mark: Is it easier or harder to get an SBA loan on a new business vs. an existing business? How about if the existing biz for sale is negative trending or barely making a profit (a turnaround)?

Reg: Securing financing for a new business or an existing one (acquisition) will bring their own, very different, challenges. Some banks will only lend for a acquisitions and won't touch startups. An acquisition with forthcoming financials will lead to a speedy closing. On the other hand, underwriting an acquisition might present a line of questioning about methods used in booking revenues and expenses on the profit and loss statement. The balance sheet will require in-depth underwriting that could lead to requiring significant amounts of supporting documents. In some cases, it might actually be more favorable to submit to financing for a startup!

A brief story about a turnaround. It wasn't long ago that we placed $1.5 million in financing for an independent home entertainment business. The company was founded in the 60's and had decades of excellent performance. During the downturn of our economy the company faced very tough, and never experienced before, financial challenges. In fact, the financials from the company showed over five years of negative performance. We performed an in-depth analysis of the financials for the last 10 years, following the financial performance from its positive position through it's downturn. Among other research performed, we delved into the independent home entertainment business sector and found the pattern of our client's business clearly reflected that which had taken place in the sector at large. Pulling all the research together and building a five-year projection a business plan was constructed that supported the reason for the downturn and further established that the company would, with enhanced sales and marketing efforts, rebound in short time.

Startups don't bring any baggage along. A concise presentation in the business plan's financial model could very well prove to be more simple than examining the financials of an acquisition.

Mark: Many years ago I had an individual I was working with in the Midwest that was undercapitalized to do that particular business. A family member stepped up to the plate and offered up cash infusion and signed the paperwork with them as a guarantor...Still common practice?

Reg: We are often working with customer's whose family has contributed to the cash injection requirement. There are varying ways to design a corporate structure in cases when family, friend, or investor have contributed cash. The design depends on how much the contributing family member wants to be involved and/or recognized in the business enterprise.

Mark: Many of the millennials do not have the liquidity or net worth to qualify for a franchise. I'm starting to see franchisors offer up internal financing again. This was pretty common practice 30 years ago. That's how Jaye and I got into our first franchise. Do you see this coming more into play?

Reg: Internal franchisor financing can be quite the slippery slope. After all, a franchise system is in the business of promoting and selling franchises, not in being a financing facility. Taking the eye off the ball and venturing into another arena can prove to be a very big mistake. A franchisor should not offer in-house financing when there are companies whose wheelhouse is financing.

For the more than 300 franchise companies we have represented, we operate seamlessly; in a way, similar to being the financing department "down the hallway." We work extremely close with the franchise organization, making every effort to take on their culture and vision.

The goal is always to ensure the financing journey is as free from bumps as possible. Educating the entrepreneur in how to arrive financially safe so they can grow their business, is our mission.

Mark: How do folks get in touch with someone at your company?

Reg: The phone number for Direct Connect Ventures ("DCV") is 805-449-2411. We are located in the Pacific time zone and will always answer the phone during business hours. I invite you to visit our website at www.DCV-INC.com to learn more about our company. A direct contact at DCV is Anthony Byrd. His email address is Anthony@DCV-INC.com.

FRANCHISOR FINANCING

When I went into franchising back in the 1980s, it was very commonplace for the franchisor to have an internal capital company that would actually finance part of your project. In effect, they would act as the bank. Gradually, this sort of financing disappeared.

But today, we're seeing many people in their 40s or 50s who want to get into business but don't have the financial wherewithal. In response, some franchisors have once again begun offering internal loans. There are only a small handful of them right now that are offering that. I do think we'll see more and more as time marches on as it's the only way some people are going to be able to get into business, because they don't have equity in their house, they haven't saved anything and they don't have a 401(k) worth much of anything.

So how do you find out who offers franchisor financing? This information can usually be found in the franchise's federal disclosure documents or through someone like me. The availability of these types of loans shouldn't be the main reason for anybody to buy a franchise, but it certainly is a nice benefit.

Here are a few franchise companies that currently offer internal financing:

- Lawn Doctor
- Budget Blinds
- Paul Davis Emergency Services

Franchisors base their lending decisions on your credit score, your equity, your drive, your ambition and how you present yourself. They're also going to look at the same financial parameters that an SBA lender would look at.

ADDITIONAL FINANCIAL CONSIDERATIONS

The most critical piece of financial advice I can give to any potential franchisee is this: Don't overextend yourself. During your financial assessment, make sure you have plenty of money for your family to live on during your "ramp up" phase and have your family budget nailed down. Don't mix business money with personal money, because the first thing you're going to do is to use that money earmarked for your business to make your mortgage payment at the expense of your marketing budget for the month

Also avoid partnerships; they usually don't work. Why not?

If the business is successful, each partner thinks he or she is doing the 70 percent of the heavy lifting. If it's not working, he or she is still doing 70 percent of the heavy lifting. Go solo. The risk might seem greater, but you're actually going to be happier when you're the captain of your own ship (The only partner I would ever trust would be my wife of 33 years).

Another potentially dangerous situation arises when a husband buys a business for his wife. Most husbands will buy a franchise that *they* think is right, avoiding input from the spouse. If the wife is going to be running it, shouldn't she be part of the evaluation process? That is the only way this kind of "gift" has a chance of success.

A similar caveat must be given when a son has a business bought for him by his father. This kind of situation has a fighting chance to succeed when the son signs a promissory note and agrees to pay his dad back with interest. Unfortunately, this is a rarity: Most sons don't appreciate what they're being given. Most crash and burn. As a matter of fact, I've only had one work.

FAMILY ASSESSMENT

The family unit has always played a crucial role in the development of society. Indeed, from the beginning of recorded history through to contemporary books, films and television shows, we've placed the concept of family front and center in the culture of mankind. It is also at the center of our daily lives, providing the kind of emotional sustenance and support that is available nowhere else. For many people, if not most, family members are the nucleus around which we focus our long-term aspirations and day-to-day goals.

Just as it plays a central role in our private lives, the family is also critically important in a business sense. Do family members approve of your livelihood? Do they support your business goals? Are they there for you when things go well and not so well?

These types of questions take on added significance when

you are about to step out on your own and when you open
the doors of your own business, such as a franchise.

THE IMPACT ON YOUR FAMILY

Face the facts: If you've been working for someone else and
now you're going out on your own, it is going to have an
impact on your family and you'll need to have a serious conversation with all your family members. Everybody needs to
be on board with what you're about to embark upon.

It's a lot of work, launching a business. There is no paycheck,
no benefits, so everybody has to be supportive of dad or mom
as they embark on their new venture. There may not be a new
car for your spouse that year; maybe Johnny will need to skip
football camp. You might be embarking on the most difficult
venture you have ever taken on.

Everybody has to give something up, including the person
doing the business. If you want to succeed, you've got to sacrifice. Ask yourself: What are you willing to give up? Seriously...
What is it?

THE IDEAL FINANCIAL SCENARIO

The "perfect storm" is when one spouse is running the day-
to-day operations of the franchise, while the other spouse is
still working at his or her job and getting medical benefits.
That way, the couple isn't pressed for immediate cash flow. In
this happy scenario, the "working" spouse is supportive and
many times working in the franchise in an admin capacity.

The family relationship remains strong and the franchisee has a great shot at becoming successful.

Conversely, the worst scenario is if neither spouse is working and they're tight on cash to begin with: kids in college, high credit card debt, monthly car payments, etc. You're looking at a potentially ruinous financial situation.

In my role as a consultant, this second scenario makes me nervous. To this applicant, I probably would say, "I don't think you're ready to do this. Focus your energies on finding a job."

Another key family factor is something I call the "Leave it to Beaver" Syndrome (or LITBS). This unfortunate situation is usually found in the non-supportive spouse who's not from an entrepreneurial background.

In the course of interviewing, I'll ask both spouses about what their parents did for a living. The LITBS sufferer came from a situation where dad worked, while mom usually stayed home and cared for the house and kids. For the husband, it was a Monday through Friday workweek, nine to five, and he worked 35 years for the same company. That company covered medical insurance as well as a monthly pension. Upon retirement, they threw a big party and presented him with a gold-inscribed watch. That's what the LITBS spouse is used to and such a mindset can be a true stumbling block when a franchise is under consideration by a family.

The reality in the job market is that people are flipping jobs every three to five years. And for those who haven't adjusted to this reality, finances can be a problem. As a case in point, consider a fellow that I'm in touch with on LinkedIn. He was a regional manager in the Midwest for a large national retailer. After another subpar year for the company, he lost his position. He's in his 50s, and we sat down and talked about a franchise. You'd think, in a position like his, that he probably made a decent salary. Yes, but he couldn't even put $100,000 together to invest in a business. He has no equity in his property, and his wife suffered from LITBS. Once the reality of the situation dawned on him, we eliminated franchising pretty quickly. Because his franchise option was out of reach, he finally secured a position with another retail outfit.

This man's problem—one that affected his business decisions—was that he didn't save any money. So this is a question I ask my clients and one that I'll ask you right here: How much do you need to retire on? In my experience, most people have no idea.

The "sweet spot", in my opinion, is to put yourself in a position to have access to $100,000 a year and have a net worth of $3 million or more. When many of us graduated college, a million dollars was a lot of money. Making $100,000 a year was a lot of money. The reality today is that those dollar amounts are probably what you're going to need to keep your boat afloat.

FINAL THOUGHTS

If your family is resistant to your dream of owning a franchise, vehemently resistant, you're probably not going to get them onboard with your plan. You'll need to do something else. Do not go down this path because it could be a disaster. You can't start a business and live in a house where you'll need to constantly walk on eggshells.

Case in point: My wife was so angry with me about our first franchise business that she was ready to leave halfway through training in California. We did get through it and we make fun of it now. Truthfully, my dream wasn't her dream and I dragged her into it. Part of the reason we came to be successful is that she became emotionally invested in it. In our franchise, she took the front of the house and I took the back.

Yes, family assessment can be a challenge. But if you can cast an objective eye on the people who share your daily life, assessing your family should be relatively simple. More challenging is the next assessment: the personal one.

PERSONALITY ASSESSMENT

What type of personality do you have?

- Are you a "people-person"?
- Do you like to organize?
- Can you do consultative selling?
- Do people work with you or for you?
- Would you say you're a "sky-is-the-limit" kind of individual? Or do you get discouraged easily?

Now that we've looked at the financial assessment and the family assessment, we turn to the topic of who *you* are. Yes, your financial health is important, as is the willingness of your family to get behind you as you embark on this new business challenge. But ultimately, it all comes down to one person: you.

Although many people disregard its role in the ultimate

decision, your personality is a crucial factor in understanding if you're the right kind of person to be a franchisee and, if so, which franchise is best for you.

NAVIGATING YOUR ABILITIES

The franchisors know who they're looking for. They're very clear in what they tell consultants such as myself. Some go a step further: About 30 percent of the franchise companies I work with use a company like Franchise Navigator to develop a behavioral profile to help them screen potential franchisees. Among the several companies using profile assessments developed by Franchise Navigator are Window Genie, Arc Point Laboratories and Supercuts.

Originated by Craig Slavin, these personality assessment profiles are incredibly insightful. I recently had a conversation with Craig, in which he discussed personality types, which I'll now share you.

Mark: How many franchisors have you worked with?

Craig: During my 40-year span in franchising I have worked with hundreds of companies all over the world in virtually every industry. From small start-ups to very large, mature organizations including Sears, Shell, AT&T, Nestle, Ingersoll-Rand, Apple, Disney and Hewlett-Packard. Currently, we are directly working with over 170 brands domestically and over 30 internationally.

Mark: What do franchisors have you do for them?

Craig: It actually depends on the client's needs. Some of them are start-up franchisors and we develop the entire franchise system for them via Franchise Architects. If they are already franchising, we benchmark their existing franchise operators using Franchise Navigator, our proprietary Skills, Values and Behavioral Assessment tool and methodology, and create for them a specific High Performer Profile of what their "ideal" franchisee profile looks like. We then guide them through the recruitment and attraction strategy process to ensure they are attracting candidates that resemble their profile. Selling a franchise to the "wrong type of person" is worse than not selling one at all. All of our clients migrate to a "profile-based" growth strategy instead of "casting a wide net" and then trying to figure out which ones they should select and award their franchises to. As a result, many of our clients have grown their market share significantly because they are selecting the right people with the "right stuff" to grow and expand their business. Further, many of our clients have seen significant increases in actual unit level sales by their franchise operators. The impact of having the right people has increased sales between 12 and 38 percent for many of our clients.

Mark: Why is it important that I have every prospective franchisee that I work with take your 10 minute survey?

Craig: I believe three of the most important questions we ask ourselves are: What am I going to do? Where am I going to do it? And with whom am I going to do it with? Investigating a franchise or business ownership is one of those three. No one wakes up in the morning and says, "I am going to buy a franchise today." People generally seek self-employment after something has happened in their life. Either they have been downsized, let go, or their financial security is either at risk or they are seeking greater security and rewards than what they are experiencing.

What makes this process even more confusing is that people, as a whole, are not totally objective with themselves: their strengths, weaknesses and style, and whether self-employment is even a good idea for them. Our Navigator Assessment quickly and accurately identifies who that person is. It is a Skills, Values and Behavioral Assessment that has no preconceived notion of the individual. It clearly and quickly identifies who they are and where they are in their lives at the time they take the assessment. Knowledge is power and the fully automated Navigator Survey System will instantly provide incredible insights and power into an individual's strengths and weaknesses by creating their own Personal Source Code. Just like computer software, everybody is wired differently and before a person makes a critical decision they need to look inside, at themselves, first.

Mark: Describe the four basic profile types.

Craig: The Franchise Navigator categorizes behavior into four distinct profiles:

- Accomplisher, with the characteristics of drive, motivation and goal orientation
- Influencer, with the characteristics of sales, communication, image and prestige
- Associator, with people skills, tolerance and acceptance
- Contributor, with leadership, contribution and selflessness

Every person has a dominant profile and at least one subordinate profile. The dominant tends to be the driving force; the subordinate profiles support and reinforce the dominant profile. Based on the results, they will be able to see which is their highest score and Dominant Profile and which are their Subordinate Profiles. This identifies what motivates a person and what rewards they are seeking in life.

Launched in 1997, after 10 years of researching personality profile types, our team of statisticians and behavioral experts made the determination that what is important are the values an individual holds close to his or her heart. The Franchise Navigator identifies and quantifies an individual's value system.

Mark: Which profile type can sell?

Craig: Influencers. People with scores of 40 percent or below are generally sales adverse. At approximately 55 percent, their sales skills start developing, and at 92 percent, they end up becoming very manipulative individuals. Influencer scores will always dominate over Associator and Contributor scores. Dominant Influencers do not do well in a business model where back-end work, reports and accounting need to be done. They are better suited for sales and marketing positions or businesses, or where the back office is computerized and it will take less effort on their part. Influencers are not strong at time management, people development and business acumen because they lack patience and attention span, especially if the scores exceed 85 percent. Income, prestige and recognition are motivating factors for high scoring Influencers.

Mark: Which can manage people?

Craig: Associators. People with Associator scores between 70 and 80 percent reflect a person who is amiable and accommodating with strong work ethics. They have an attention to detail and are dependable, loyal, compassionate and customer service-oriented. Scores below 45 percent can indicate an anti-social individual. Success and prestige are not important to them. Safety, security and being accepted are. They are also sales adverse as they avoid conflict and won't want to do or say anything that will potentially alienate them from being liked or accepted. Associators tend to work well with smaller groups of people such as what you would find in many franchised business models.

Mark: Please share with us a common profile and break it down. What types of business models would be good for this person?

Craig: There are many different combinations of profiles. A Dominant Accomplisher with Associator and Contributor Subordinates is generally, depending on the scores, an "empire builder" and will want to own multiple locations. A Dominant Associator with Accomplisher and Contributor Subordinates will excel in a single unit franchise with a smaller group of employees and a more routine type of business. This is the model of a cookie store or even like a Starbucks.

WHAT FRANCHISORS ARE SAYING

It was Mark who introduced me to the Franchise Navigator

after I expressed concerns about a number of candidates who showed interest in Window Genie, but I felt weren't the right fit.

After 21 years in business, Window Genie's M.O. is to "award" not "sell" franchises. We're not interested in going into business with individuals that don't fit the system; it doesn't benefit either party. Proudly operating with over 80 owners in 27 states, Window Genie is built on the strength of our franchise partners who follow the system and are passionate about the business.

Mark's extensive knowledge of buyer motivation has been an incredible resource to Window Genie for many years. After Mark explained the function and purpose of the Navigator tool, I was sure this was what we needed to improve our franchise development process moving forward. The Navigator is now THE go-to tool for helping us understand which candidates fit our model and who has the highest likelihood of succeeding.

Having the ability to "weed out" the wrong owners is crucial to successful growth as a franchise. This is probably the best thing we've done for our franchise development process. I wish I'd known about this tool ten years ago!

Richard Nonelle,
Founder & CEO, Window Genie

Here is the link to the Franchise Navigator test: www.franchisenavigator.com/connectme

For $49.95 you receive a Personal Profile Report, a Workbook entitled, "How To Evaluate A Franchise," and access to approved vendors/suppliers and discounted rates for their Certified Navigator Life & Business Coaches, which you can check out at www.navigatorcoach.com.

WHAT THE RESULTS MEAN

In a nutshell, the profile is going to tell me—as a consultant— if you have the ability to sell, build something, run a small team and keep a crew together. They are all key indicators that come out in the test.

So, think about a high-profile franchise company, taking in 1,000 or more Internet leads per month. Many of these leads are not qualified because they just don't have the skill sets. Wouldn't *you* want to work with candidates who have at least been vetted through a personality profile?

Keep in mind that these assessments aren't perfect, but they tend to be about 85 percent accurate when done right.

There are two crucial skills that determine the best franchise fits for an individual: sales and management. Let's take a look at how these skills are suited to particular types of businesses.

THE FIRST CRUCIAL SKILL: SALES

If you can sell, but not manage, and if you are a true sales professional, there are heavily sales-based franchises you can succeed in. Many of these are one-man bands, just the individual franchisee handling the business. It could be a professional coaching business like Sandler Sales Training or Focal Point. It could be a direct marketer such as Money Mailer (coupons delivered via mail) or Welcomemat (a modern-day version of Welcome Wagon).

There are many more franchises that are made just for the sales professional. They require low investment levels, usually with working capital under $100,000 and many times under $75,000. In most of these types of businesses, you don't need to have an outside office; you can work out of your house. And these are usually Monday through Friday businesses.

Let's look a bit closer at Money Mailer, a merge-mail program that allows vendors to advertise in a single packet that's sent to residences. Commonly, you'll see coupons for bagel bakeries, sandwich shops, workout facilities, pizza joints, etc. So, as a franchisee, you're going to different vendors to sell them on the concept of couponing with you. You'll be out on the road much of the time, calling on clients, because Money Mailer publishes about 12 mailings a year.

What about sales leads? A sales company like this may sometimes provide you with leads. They may do some work for you and set up some appointments in the beginning; they may do some dialing right from corporate headquarters. But usually, after that first 30 days, you're going to be on your own even though they will have set up the table for you.

THE SECOND CRUCIAL SKILL: MANAGING

If you can manage, but not sell, you want a franchise that is less sales-focused. As an example, let's look at the residential cleaning business. Instead of cold calling, you're doing some type of external advertising. It could be Google AdWords, it could be a Money Mailer, a Val Pack or it could be getting a phone call off your company-marked vehicle. This takes a cold call and turns it into an informational or warm call.

It could also be a painting business or a handyman business. We find with a number of the service-based brands, they actually have a national call center through which all your calls are filtered. There's a charge for this type of service, a couple of percentage points on top of your royalties, but they will actually set appointments for you.

If you're passionate about your business, it's very easy to talk to people about it, solve their problem, save them some money and offer them some good old-fashioned customer service. It's not like you're out there trying to sell them life insurance or magazines door-to-door.

Another option is to have a retail franchise in which you do advertising and customers come to you. Examples include Supercuts, Great Clips, a workout place, and many others such as fast food and massage places. These types of businesses typically cost $175,000 to $550,000.

Unfortunately, these will cost more money than the sales-driven franchises we just discussed; remember, many of those usually require less than $100,000 all in. For service brands, the amount can vary depending on your investment in equipment and inventory. For example, in Window Genie's case, they want you to have the first year's worth of marketing money rolled into your all-in number. That's $48,000 alone. You'll need about $165,000 to get started when every expense is factored in.

With a retail concept, time plays an important role. Think about all the time that goes into finding a location (with the help of the franchisor) and negotiating (again with the help of the franchisor). Then there's the whole build-out phase. And don't forget, you've got to go get trained. So it's a minimum of eight months from the time you begin to move forward until you get your doors open. In that same time frame, new franchisees will be cash-positive in a service model that's home-based.

There is an alternative, however. With some of these retail operations, the model is semi-absentee. You might be able to keep your day job. This is an excellent choice for that person who's risk-averse. You keep your day job, get the first location open, take the profit from the first one and put it into the second one. Maybe by year four or five, you've got three locations open. Maybe at the end of year five, the cash is flowing, at which point you can transition out of your day job, replacing all of your salary with income from your franchises. This, by the way, would be the classic model for Super Cuts or Meineke Car Care Centers.

ALL OR NOTHING

If you can both manage and sell, you can succeed in almost any franchise.

I don't see that person very often. Usually, people are good at one or the other. When I come across one that's good at both, that's exciting because it opens up all kinds of doors.

The converse is true with the individual who can neither manage nor sell.

That person is pretty much stuck with a "field of dreams" business: build it and they will come. At least, that's what the hope would be. If you can't manage, you can't manage. If you can't sell, you can't sell. So I would say to that group of architects, engineers, IT people and accountants who can't do either of those, stay in private practice.

In reality, these non-qualified people usually don't get very far in the application process. Remember, in my consultancy, before I send you to a franchisor, I've talked to you for a minimum of 45 minutes to let you know what I do. You're then going to tell me about yourself. I'm going to have you fill out some paperwork and take the Franchise Navigator test, and then I'm going to spend between an hour-and-a-half and two hours with you on the phone asking you a ton of questions. So we've spent almost three hours on the phone before we even talk about a franchise brand!

Next, I'll usually roll out six to eight franchise brands. We'll whittle the list down and I will tell you everything I know about the company including a realistic all-in number. We'll talk about some of their unique or universal value propositions. What makes this widget better? What makes this company desirable? Am I seeing larger territories, more money spent on marketing? What are they doing differently that others are not?

Remember, in franchising, the whole idea is to steal market share from the independents. The independents have a hard time competing with the franchise. As we stated earlier, as a franchisee you are able to step right in to that nice situation in which time- and money-consuming processes are all created in advance for you.

WHO'S LOOKING FOR WHAT?

To some extent, franchisors are all looking for the same thing. They're looking for somebody who's a team player, who can follow a process and follow a system. That's why franchisors love military people: They know how to listen, they're team players and they know how to follow a system.

What about you? Ask yourself what you are looking for. It's up to you to assess that. You've got to ask yourself what's most important to you. Is it money? Is it passion? Is it fun? Is it getting wealthy? Or are you trying to improve your quality of life? All of them? Something else?

If I'm working with somebody under 45, generally speaking, all that matters is the money. When I work with someone in their mid-50s, it's often a person who's been a road warrior, away from home 30 weeks out of the year; this person wants to improve his quality of life. He's tired of being a million-mile flight member with United Airlines. Many people hate what they're doing and they want to have some fun; they want to be passionate about what they do. That comes out as a very high benchmark for people over 55. But truthfully, we're all looking for something different.

Here are the types of questions I ask my clients and you should be asking yourself:

- As it relates to business, what do you like to do and not like to do?
- How tolerant of risk are you?
- Do you work better with men or women?
- Do you speak a second language?
- What jobs did you have as a kid?
- What civic or service organizations do you belong to?

Some people are looking for a business that doesn't exist. And what doesn't exist? The perfect business. I have never seen one. There just aren't any, and if there are, get in line behind me.

Many times, people just don't want to work very hard. This is where I must remind you that franchising is not for the meek. In the beginning, you're probably going to work harder on this than you did on your day job.

FINAL THOUGHTS

From my perspective as a consultant, I'm not going to let clients get into a business that they hate. That's not what this is all about. This is supposed to make things better.

Here's a pet peeve of mine. I've been working with a client and we're heading towards the finish line; we've narrowed it down to two companies and the client asks me, "Which one of these two would you do?"

I don't have any answer for that because it doesn't matter what I say. What's the best for the client? What's going to get you where you want to go? How much do you need to make? Do you need to have your weekends off? Are you coaching soccer? What kind of things do you like to do when you're not working?

Those answers can only come from you.

PART TWO

FIND AND APPLY

—

FRANCHISING BASICS

This part of the book will focus on how to find the right franchise for your situation then look at the ins and outs of applying. It can be a long and complex process, so first we need to step back and learn a little more about how franchises work.

TAPPING INTO DISCLOSED INFO

Investing in a franchise is different than looking at a mom-and-pop business in a number of ways. To begin with, to get the information you need about a non-franchised business, you have to be a kind of Sherlock Holmes tracking down all the clues you need to make a decision.

With a franchise, much of the important information that you are going to get will be contained in a Franchise Disclosure Document (FDD). It's a treasure trove of facts and figures about the operations of the franchise you're interested in, but it can be a bit daunting when you go through it the first time. They typically run, in PDF format, upwards of 250 pages. Here's a sampling of what you'll find in the FDD's table of contents:

- The franchisor and any parents, predecessors and affiliates
- Business experience
- Litigation
- Bankruptcy
- Royalties and national ad fees
- Estimated initial investment
- Franchisee's obligations
- Territory size

And this is not an all-inclusive list! As you can see, the document tells you what it's going to cost you to get in, what you get for your money and what the franchisor expects you to do. It's also going to give you last year's P & L and balance sheet on the parent company, along with a full roster of franchisees: names, addresses and phone numbers.

Essentially, it's a medium-sized book filled with some legalese. For that reason, I recommend that you retain a franchise attorney to help you understand what the FDD is telling you.

[A side note: I've actually had clients pull FDDs from the Web and start calling franchisees with the intention of pumping them for information before they even talk to the franchisor. Not a good idea. Nobody is going to talk to you. You know why? All the franchisors have a password. If you're not playing by their rules, their franchisees aren't going to talk to you. You're an utter stranger. For all they know, you could be a potential competitor.]

WHY YOU NEED A FRANCHISE ATTORNEY

Recently, I had the opportunity to speak with Chamise Sibert, Managing Partner of Sibert Law, a law firm with deep experience in the franchise business. Here's her perspective on the value that a franchise attorney brings to the table.

Mark: I plan to purchase a franchise and my neighbor is a real estate attorney. Why shouldn't I use him or her to review the franchise agreement?

Chamise: Although there are lots of attorneys practicing in the United States, franchising is a specialty practice area that touches on federal and state law. An attorney experienced in franchising can help you understand general contract principles as well as franchise specific federal and state rules and regulations. While general contract laws apply to each legal contract, franchising has its own unique nuisances. Many general practitioners or attorneys with experience in other areas will review a franchise agreement with only general contract rules in mind. A franchise attorney will focus on these issues, but will also zero in on issues that might potentially affect your franchise.

A general practice attorney might spend hours editing or challenging certain provisions of the agreement that are standard in the industry, such as confidentiality or the assignment of a specific territory to a potential franchisee. A franchise attorney, on the other hand, will recognize that confidentiality is paramount in a franchise relationship because the franchisor will share potentially proprietary information with franchisees. As a new franchisee, you will receive training on franchise-specific methods and trade secrets related to operation, sales, etc. This information is not offered to the general public and there are steep consequences if you breach this confidentiality. While standard contracts may negotiate these terms, in franchising it is commonplace to restrict access to such information because of its sensitive nature. It can be helpful to have an experienced set of eyes review the agreement based upon industry standards, particularly if you are new to franchising or business ownership in general.

The franchise agreement is the first of many contracts that you would counter as a new business owner. Federal law requires that every franchisor issue the franchise disclosure document (FDD) to prospective franchisee; however, the federal government does not require that franchisors submit the FDD to a federal agency or third-party organization for review or approval. The federal government also does not screen franchisors, so companies may offer franchises without hiring competent legal counsel to draft or review their FDD. Therefore, it is important that you hire a franchise attorney to ensure that the FDD adheres to federal guidelines and state laws. Franchise law is ever changing and an experienced franchise attorney will help you navigate the ins and outs of this area of the law.

Franchising can be compared to your relationship with your

physician. While a general practitioner can help you if you have an upset stomach or leg sprain, when you have chest pains, you consult with a cardiologist because they specialize in heart conditions. A franchise attorney operates in a similar fashion by focusing on a niche area of the law. The franchise relationship is also the starting point for other day-to-day business relationships such as your relationship with vendors, landlords and employees. Within one franchise deal, you might sign a real estate lease, rent equipment under a commercial lease, use third-party software and sign a software licensing agreement, and hire employees under an employment agreement. A general practitioner might not realize that a breach of a commercial lease could also affect your franchise or vice a versa.

An experienced franchise attorney can walk you through different phases of franchise start up and development, as well as expansion of your franchise to multiple locations, acquiring additional territories and even a franchise transfer or sale. By establishing a relationship with a franchise attorney on the front end, you are creating a partnership that can assist you in building a successful business.

Mark: Why do I need a franchise attorney if franchisors are not willing to change the agreement?

Chamise: A franchise review provides potential franchisees with the detailed analysis of the franchise agreement terms, conditions and obligations. It is designed to help you fully understand what is expected of you as a franchisee, and what you should expect in return for your investment in the business. In becoming a franchisee, you are about to invest a large portion of your time, resources and finances into a new business venture. We recommend that clients engage a franchise attorney in order to understand all of the contract terms up front. In some instances, there are items that a franchisor may be flexible on in order to expand the brand. A franchise attorney will guide you to these areas of the franchise agreement and explain areas that are potentially non-negotiable.

As a franchisee, you are responsible for assembling a team of professionals to guide you through this process and to protect your interests. A franchise attorney can identify potential legal pitfalls or items that you should understand before you sign the agreement. Our firm offers a unique perspective because we have worked on both sides of the fence with franchisors and franchisees. A commonly expressed concern of many franchisors is that modifying a franchise agreement might have a ripple effect because one change might impact another provision, particularly if you're in a registration state. On the other side of the coin, a common frustration for potential franchisees is that the franchise agreement was drafted solely by the franchisor to protect its interest.

An experienced franchise attorney is familiar with the parts of the agreement that are written in stone. For example, franchisors are not likely to negotiate concrete provisions such as trademark use or a location's color scheme because of the potential effect on the franchise brand. Your franchise attorney will point out sections that may be open to compromise such as start-up dates and other preopening requirements, territory size, future rights to expand, retail location specifics, development deadlines, expansion rights, or local marketing fees and requirements.

If a specific section of the agreement is vague or unclear, an attorney can help you clarify that language with the franchisor. Counsel can also help you identify personal issues or special circumstances that could affect your franchise development such as seasonal conditions, personal background or prior experience in a specific industry, competition within your area from similar businesses, etc. In our experience, presenting these issues to a franchisor not only educates them on your specific needs, but it also helps both parties agree upon fair and reasonable contract terms.

We also assist clients by highlighting items that they might otherwise overlook, but that could potentially affect their business in the future. We often caution our clients to consult with us frequently during the first few years of business in order to avoid mistakes that could put their franchise in jeopardy. No owner wants to invest years and money into a business only to find out that he committed an "accidental franchise default" and is in danger of losing his franchise. While federal law outlines franchise rules and regulations, there are best business practices that cannot be found in any law book. We can help you understand issues that are not captured on paper.

Mark: Can I negotiate the size of my franchise territory for the price of additional franchises if I purchase more than one territory?

Chamise: It really depends on the franchisor, but it does not hurt to try. Some franchises will negotiate the territory price if you purchase multiple territories. In return, the franchise might require a good-faith deposit for each additional territory or that you sign a development schedule for the second or third territories. Other franchisees might be eager to expand into a specific area of the country or to introduce the franchise brand to a new customer base. If so, then this is a prime opportunity for you to request a territory size that will help you develop an undeveloped or under-developed area.

Franchisors will often devote lots of time carving out a franchise territory that is a win-win for both parties. Factors that might influence territory size and shape are where the franchise candidate resides, the franchisee's familiarity and knowledge of the territory, population density, and the candidate's personal ties to the community, demographics and other unique factors. The key point for you to remember is that you want to identify a franchise territory that fits you now and in the future because most franchise agreements lock in your territory for a term of five to 20 years. If you focus only on the market that you will serve today, then you might miss out on opportunities tomorrow. Remember, as a business owner, you must also bounce between present and future business needs. It also does not serve you well to select a massive territory that consumes all of your resources, which prohibits you from establishing a successful base because you were stretched too thin. Franchising, and any business for that matter, is about relationships and your ability to reach your target market. As a resident of Dallas, you might not want to select a territory that is five hours away unless you have ties to that area and have a strong marketing plan. Typically, a targeted approach is a much better fit in the long run and will contribute to your success.

Mark: Will we review the FDD and the actual contract that I will sign?

Chamise: Yes, we will review the current FDD, which includes the franchise agreement that you plan to sign. A full review includes the entire document, which provides the picture of the franchise relationship. Your franchise agreement should include the names of all persons that will be franchisees. If you have created a corporation or LLC, the franchise agreement should list that entity as the franchisee. It should also identify your territory, the schedules for future locations (if available), and any additional specifics for your franchise. An example of these additional documents might include a personal guaranty or software licensing agreement.

Mark: What is a registration state and how is it different from a non-registration state?

Chamise: The simple answer is that a registration state requires that a franchisor to "register" its franchise with a specific state agency before it offers franchises for sale in that state. Presently, there are 14 registration states that require this extra step. The Federal Trade Commission regulates the franchise industry on the federal level and each state is responsible for crafting rules that govern franchise sales within its borders. A registration state requires, at a minimum, an additional FDD review and approval process, registration fees, surety bonds and compliance with the annual renewal process in order to continue to offer franchises within that state. In non- registration states, franchisors might not be required to submit their FDD to that state, but they will need to ensure that the franchise complies with other state laws. The good news is that as a franchisee, you are not typically responsible for this part of the process. (Please note that while most single-unit franchise owners are not required to register on the state level, some exceptions exist with area developers in specific states.)

You should verify with an experienced franchise attorney that the franchise is in compliance with federal and state laws in registration and non-registration states. A few years ago, we reviewed an agreement and discovered that it complied with federal but not state guidelines for initial and ongoing monthly fees. When we presented this issue to the franchisor, they realized their oversight and withdrew the franchise opportunity in order to correct this issue. If our client had moved forward with that franchise and the state learned of the noncompliance, our client's franchise might have been invalidated and she could have faced an uphill battle in order to obtain a refund of her initial investment of fees and other expenses. She was grateful to avoid this potential headache and the chance that she might have lost her investment or faced other legal consequences.

If the FDD is still being reviewed in a registration state, the franchisor is prohibited from offering the franchise to any potential candidate. So please request that the franchisor provide proof of registration status if you plan to open a franchise within the 14 registration states.

Mark: If I am working with an attorney, do I need to review the agreement?

Chamise: Yes, we recommend that our clients review the entire FDD at least once or even twice. The average FDD is between 200 to 300 pages and contains a vast amount of information on the franchise executive team, franchise history, and its predecessors or affiliates. It also contains information on the core franchise model, operations, vendors and suppliers, marketing territory, initial and ongoing fees, trademark registration, and a separate legal contract that outlines obligations of the franchisor and franchisee. Because of the length of the document, past clients confessed only scanning the pages, while others would admit to falling asleep before reaching the end! As the business owner, you need to be familiar with the agreement. It also helps to review the agreement before consulting with our firm so that we can answer any questions and clarify any items. While we assist in reviewing the legal issues, you must also understand the business-related items and accounting issues.

Mark: Can you help a client incorporate his or her business?

Chamise: Absolutely. We often help clients register the corporation or limited liability company, register a trade name or obtain industry-specific business licenses. We also provide business-related legal services such as contract drafting and review, negotiating vendor agreements, drafting shareholder agreements and commercial real estate leases, structure franchise deals to acquire additional territories or even transfer a franchise due to retirement, etc.

Mark: What are my next steps?

Chamise: Please reach out for us for an initial consultation so that we might discuss your needs. Because we tailor our services to each client, we are confident that we can assist you regardless of where you are if you franchising process—start up, expansion or sale.

Mark: What other information should I know before we start?

Chamise: The last thing I will close with seems the most obvious, but it still needs to be said. We have one main request of each client, that they are completely honest and upfront so that we can provide competent legal advice. If you plan to exit the franchise within three years, even though it has a 10-year term, then tell us that so we can review your exit strategy when reviewing the agreement. We could also assist you in creating a customized exit strategy by incorporating a no-fee transfer clause into the agreement, or structure a succession plan to help you make a smooth transition to a new owner.

Some past clients did not disclose certain things, like they were buying it for their son or daughter to operate. When we discovered this arrangement, we saw it was in violation of the franchise agreement. Had we not discovered this in time, it could have cost our client over $10,000 to resolve and he would have been in danger of losing his franchise. So this very kindhearted father, who was trying to provide for future generations, could've made a simple, yet costly business mistake. We believe that open and honest communication at each stage is crucial to receiving the best legal advice for your situation. Please remember that the franchise relationship and the franchise itself is a living, breathing organism. As a franchise grows and changes—trust me, you want it to change and adapt in today's world—the relationship will be different in year one versus year four.

An experienced franchise attorney will help you understand and potentially capitalize on the changing relationship over time. While we cannot anticipate every potential scenario, based upon our years of experience and training, we can help you identify potential issues and decide if they need to be addressed now or as the business develops. One of the most recognized examples of franchising was a restaurant that originally served burgers and fries. In the early stages, the menu contained three or four items including burgers, fries, milkshakes and carbonated beverages. Today, the typical menu of a burger franchise may contain more than 30 regular items and that does not include the endless choices of combinations. The question is no longer 'do you want fries with that?' Now employees ask if you want cheese on those fries. Chili and onions? Mild peppers? Spicy or regular fries? The possibilities are truly endless!

In today's world, people value a customer experience, much like franchisees want a custom agreement and experience. Consumers want some level of uniformity so that the restaurant in their hometown in Maine offers the same experience as the Miami location that they frequented during vacation. Likewise, franchisees want to invest in a proven business model and yet be able to serve the unique needs of their customers and community. And the franchisor has an interest in building a strong brand by providing a consistent product or experience no matter where it is offered in the country or even the world. From this idea, franchising was born and the concept of doing business was changed forever. Even though these groups seem to have different interests, there is a common thread. And working together to develop a business and a franchise brand can be a win-win for everyone: the franchisor, the franchisee and the customer.

Chamise Sibert: www.siberlaw.com

THE INITIAL CALL

To give you another taste of how you might wind your way through the process of getting a franchise, I'd like to share with you some of the ideas that I discuss on an initial call with a client. Although this is my own "script", all franchise coaches use it to some extent. Coaches will differ on some issues. For example, about 85 percent of coaches nationwide don't use a service like the Franchise Navigator. I do.

My conversations tend to run longer than many coaches. Many franchise coaches will have a 30-minute informational phone call with the client, and then based on the paperwork, start discussing specific franchise brands on that first call. I think that's wrong. Wouldn't it make more sense for someone to get to know you before diving into franchise brands?

For example, during the holiday season, a client in the Milwaukee area had narrowed his list down to two franchise brands. Both franchisors called and emailed him, and he neglected to call them back. I had to send him an e-mail: "Look, if you're busy for the holidays and there's too much going on, let me get that message back to the franchisors and we can pick that up the first week of January. The message you are sending to them right now is you're not interested or you're too busy." He was on the phone with both companies within 10 minutes.

The point is that you want to send the right message to the franchisor. I tell my clients that they are being evaluated through the whole process. Most of these companies have a discovery day. If you show up at a Supercuts discovery day in a pair of blue jeans and sandals and you haven't shaved in a month, you're probably not going to be offered a franchise. Yes...these types of things do happen!

On the initial phone call, I tell folks they're going to be nervous during the process. I tell them to look at the process through the eyes of a business owner and not through the eyes of an employee. We're going to talk about every single job that they've held. Why? It tells you a lot about a person if he tells me they started delivering newspapers in the sixth grade, that they worked through high school and college, and paid their own college tuition. We talk about their kids, their spouse. We go through that forced ranking we talked about earlier. We talk a lot about sales and managing people.

I'm going to ask them what's the biggest risk they've ever

taken in their professional career or in their personal life. We're going to talk about an exit strategy. We're going to talk about retail locations versus running a franchise out of their house. (By the way, some people can't work out of their house: there are too many distractions.)

We'll spend some time talking about the franchise disclosure document. We'll talk about franchise attorneys. I tell them the facts of life. For example, people think franchisors are going to negotiate with them. Wrong! A big, reputable company that's been around for 30 years is not going to change a comma in that franchise contract. How can they have different contracts for everybody? What's there to negotiate? Maybe the territory, but not the fees because it's a number published in the FDD.

My consultations usually run about two hours. There's a lot to go through to get to a position where I can intelligently do territory checks and show folks brands that are in their wheelhouse.

ANOTHER DECISION

Let's say you've always wanted to own a fast food franchise. That's a big step. Now you have to decide if you should go through the process alone or go to a coach. It's probably obvious which option I would recommend. In fact, it's kind of a no-brainer because most franchise coaches, myself included, charge no fees. In the interest of full disclosure, I'll tell you that I get paid by the franchisor when I successfully place a franchisee with their company.

Exercise caution in deciding which franchise coach to work with. There are a lot of them out there, way too many, but most of them have never owned a franchised business. In my opinion, to be on my side of the fence, you need to have the experience of working on the front lines of a franchised business so you can understand what empathy means, and maybe worked on the franchisor side, too. In addition to my experience as a franchisee, I did franchise development for two companies—Spectrum Home Services and Fibrenew—as well as pre-training for all their new franchisees. All told, I have close to 30 years of combined experience on all three sides.

Now that you know the ABCs of the franchise world, it's time to move on to the next step: Finding a franchise that's a good fit for you.

CHOOSING A FRANCHISE

If you were to sit down at your computer or pull out your tablet and type the word "franchise" into a search engine, you'd find the number of results overwhelming. As an example, go to www.franchise.org and you'll see more than 70 *categories* of franchises, representing hundreds of different companies.

Here's a sampling of those categories:

- Accounting/Tax Services
- Advertising/Direct Mail
- Assisted Living
- ATMs
- Automotive Products and Services
- Batteries: Retail/Commercial
- Beverages
- Business Brokers
- Business/Management Consulting

- Business Services
- Campgrounds
- Car & Truck Rentals
- Check Cashing & Pawn Shops
- Chemicals and Related Products
- Children's Services
- Clothing & Shoes
- Commercial & Residential Lighting
- Computer/Electronics/Internet Services

And that's just A through C!

Go through that entire list, category by category, and chances are you'd find a franchise that would match your interests and capabilities. You'd also find the names of companies that you didn't know existed, successful franchises that provide a myriad of products and services.

Here are some other sources on the web that will give you franchise lists and information:

- www.entrepreneur.com/franchises
- www.franchising.com
- www.forbes.com/best-worst-franchises-to-buy
- www.franchiseopportunities.com
- www.sba.gov/content/franchise-businesses
- www.franchisetimes.com

A number of these sources include rankings such as "The Top 10 Franchises." My advice is to take these rankings with a grain of salt. Why some of those companies end up on these "best" lists is shrouded in mystery, although it probably has something to do with gross sales and the number of locations. This doesn't mean that these companies offer good business models. As an example, I'd point to a well-known company in the health/exercise category. This franchisor sells or closes a third of its locations every year and still made the top 50 list for years for reasons unknown. Some suspect that a given company might advertise on a specific site or publication and move up the lists that way.

There's also another way to find a franchise yourself: your life experiences. Perhaps you have a friend or relative that's involved in a particular franchise. Maybe they own a UPS Store three states over. Maybe they own a McDonald's next town over. And many times people who are customers end up becoming franchisees. But please do not make this mistake, which I'll occasionally hear from a potential client. I'll ask, "Why are you interested in this particular food business?" Answer: "We like the food." You truly need a better reason than that.

COST TO YOU: MORE THAN JUST A FRANCHISE FEE

An important proviso: When you visit a franchisor's site, they'll often mention the franchise fees. Be careful.

What they're trying to do is be like anybody else who's trying to sell something; they're trying to get you to click over for more information so they can connect you with a salesperson. Let's say, for reasons of discussion, that the franchise fee is $40,000. That's just the beginning; you're also going to need a realistic amount of working capital. With my clients, I'll usually recommend six to eight months or more.

Add equipment costs, legal fees and traveling costs to get trained, and all of a sudden the $40,000 franchise fee could very well end up costing you $165,000.

EMOTION: A NECESSARY INGREDIENT

In order for a franchise to be a good choice, it needs to appeal to you both on a rational level and an emotional level. It's easy to understand why rationality plays a role; after all, you'll be examining a slew of facts and figures, determining if you have the financial wherewithal and putting together a lot of complex puzzle pieces. But what does emotion have to do with anything? Shouldn't you be holding back your emotions and be as dispassionate as you can? I'd say that is hardly the case.

If you look at benchmark moments in your life, you would probably include getting married, having kids, buying that first house, and next, right up there, is opening a business. This decision may be one of the most emotional times of your life.

On an emotional level, you'll be frightened. Everybody gets scared during this process. It doesn't matter if you've got $20 million in the bank; you'll be just as scared as the person with $100,000. After all, your pride is on the line. It can be especially scary if you've worked for somebody else your whole life. Making a decision when you're using somebody else's money is easier than making a decision that involves your own money and your own time.

THE RATIONAL YOU

Let's say you start with a large selection of reasonable choices—perhaps eight or 10. Now it's time for the rational side to kick in; it's time to rationally think about what each franchise brand offers. It's time to consider the brand's Universal Value Proposition or UVP. Here are the questions you'll need to consider:

- Is it unique?
- Is it niche?

- Does this company make its own products?
- What is it about this brand that makes it better than others or better than a mom-and-pop operation?
- Does it have national contracts?
- Does it offer multiple profit centers, advanced training or awesome technology that saves you hours of time?

Another major consideration: territory. Does the franchise have available territories in your immediate area? You don't want to be spending what I call "windshield time" on your business. That doesn't really improve your quality of life, does it? It needs to be right there where you live.

Keep in mind, too, that every area is going to have AAA territories, AA territories, B and C territories based on household demographics. Operator A purchases part of this prime territory, the AAA territory, and Operator B picks up the rest of it. Now what's left? If you look at every urban market with a suburban area, there's going to be certain areas that stand out.

After answering all of the above UVP questions, ideally your list should contain two or three brands to start seriously exploring.

COMMON MISTAKES

There are a number of mistakes that franchise rookies often make that you must avoid. Number one: Neglecting to purchase a protected territory. What is a protected territory? If it's a retail location, the franchisor will give you a radius around the location where they can't put anybody else in, typically 2 to 4 miles. If it is a non-retail business and it's a service-based brand, the territory will be defined by zip codes. That means that if you have multiple franchise partners in an area, they can't come in and do work in your area; they actually shouldn't even be doing any direct marketing in your area. How would you like it if you purchased a franchise and the franchisor sold nine more, so there were 10 of you in a 10-mile radius? That's not good for anybody.

Case in point: A business acquaintance who owned a fast-food franchise in the Northeast. He was one of the first ones to open up in his area, but there was no protected territory defined in the contract. He had a great launch and then four years later, there were four more of these franchisees all within 3 miles of him.

This was one of several big mistakes that he made. I said, "Frank, did you make validation calls to others in the network and vet this thing out? How many people did you talk to?"

His response: Zero.

The average person would want to talk to between eight and 14 existing franchisees, talk to people that have been open varying lengths of time. It's an easy matter to get the type of information you need from the franchise or perhaps a franchisee with a similar background, or from somebody in an area that has similar demographics to where you're looking to set up shop. I once had someone validate with 52 different franchisees.

Also, my friend didn't put together a business plan. Most franchisors, if you ask, will send you a blank pro forma. They can't send you one with all the line items filled in. They can do that with you once you become a franchisee.

Another biggie: He did not attend a discovery day at the franchisor's corporate headquarters so he could meet the entire team. You want to meet the home team members. You want to see them eyeball-to-eyeball. They want to see you, too. Don't you want to see whom you are marrying for the next 10 years? Thanks to today's technology, about 10 to 15 percent of the companies will set up a virtual discovery day using a Skype-type platform.

Bottom line: My friend's business kept deteriorating. He was fortunate enough to sell it off to one of his managers and get most of his money out, but he did all the wrong things. He bought purely on emotion and didn't research anything, didn't follow logical steps.

The more established the company, the less likely you're going to be able to negotiate. Much of it's going to depend on how you present yourself and how badly they want you.

Another possibility: If it's a small company, a startup, I've been able to negotiate the right of first refusal, meaning that they have to come to you first before they give a franchise to somebody else. You usually have 10 business days to say yes or no. This is a way that you can pick up some extra zip codes. I must stress, however, that this sort of arrangement is rare.

A FINANCIAL RED FLAG

Do not work with a company that's had a bankruptcy in the past 10 years. This information will be in the FDD. Why not? Because history repeats itself. In that regard, franchising and war have a lot in common.

There's one company that I was researching recently that had a bankruptcy about 10 years ago. I discovered this by going through their FDD. They retooled their model, and their cash position seemed to be pretty good. But, based on that one bankruptcy, I would not show the brand to anyone. Just as I predicted, they have stopped selling franchises because many of the franchisees are struggling.

LEGAL RED FLAGS

In the FDD, you'll also see how many lawsuits a franchisor has been involved with. You'll get a full dossier of what the suits were all about. Do not work with a company that has a bad history of litigations. Why? Don't you want to be working with someone that likes to resolve problems?

I remember the very first FDD I looked at. I was investigating some printing companies, and ended up being awarded one. But the one that I didn't get involved with had an inch-thick list of litigation in its FDD: lawsuits from franchisees for not enforcing protected territories, failure to train, etc. That company was eliminated from my list very quickly.

Companies must disclose to you any lawsuits that are currently pending and anything going back as far as a decade that's been settled. Ideally, you really want to be working with a company where there's nothing there. I have no problem with a franchisor protecting the rights of franchisees from a rogue franchisee: someone that won't logo their vehicle, someone that won't use the vendors they're supposed to be using, etc. There's a whole list of rules that you need to be following.

As an example, let's return to my very first franchise, Postal Instant Press. When I signed on, I followed everything to the letter, installing the mandated outdoor sign, color of carpeting, countertops, wall paint, etc. Then, two years later, it all changed: the sign, the carpeting, the countertops, the paint. That's a $20,000 revamp I had to do and they gave franchisees a two-year window to complete the facelift.

While you don't want to see any litigation in a given franchisor's FDD, there are some legal actions that are understandable. Let's say the franchisor is going after a rogue franchisee that's not doing what he's supposed to do. For example, everybody else has a company-marked vehicle and this fellow is running around in a rust bucket.

If it's a brand where the employees need to be uniformed, they need to be uniformed. A rogue franchisee cannot go outside of his protected territory and work in somebody else's protected territory. That has happened to me two times; I was able to make one phone call and a cease-and-desist was issued by the franchisor to the rogue franchisee.

How many lawsuits are too many? I don't like seeing any, but it's all going to depend on how many franchisees they have. If they've got 100 franchisees, I'd hope to see no lawsuits in the FDD. If they've got 1,000, you may see a couple. This is America and people sue.

Generally speaking, when all is said and done, the franchisor doesn't want to take legal action. That will stay in the FDD for a long time.

DANGEROUS BURN RATES (ATTRITION RATES)

Avoid companies with a high burn rate. The back of the FDD will give you a roster of the amount of units that close in a given year. Using simple math, you can see how many franchisees there are, how many have gone out of business in the past year, then come up with your own burn rate.

The franchisor's FDD will give you a list of everybody that's not in the system since the last FDD was published. That would include anybody that's been terminated.

It could be a mutual termination; let's say there was a death in the family, a great personal illness, a divorce. The burn rate also includes people that have sold (or transferred) their business to somebody else.

You can also do your own investigating. You'll find the name, address and phone number in the FDD of anybody that's left the system since the previous FDD. The franchisee is not happy doing the business, they bought into a C territory, it's too hard or they've run out of money.

Sometimes young franchisors take on anybody with a pulse and a checkbook. They need to in order to survive and they'll bring the wrong people into their business. Terminations of one kind or another ensue.

If it's a business that requires someone to manage people, why would somebody who's never managed anyone before buy a cleaning franchise? If it was a business that required a great deal of professional salesmanship, why would somebody who's an engineer think they can sell and get into that business? In these cases, neither side has done their due diligence and vetted properly.

FINAL THOUGHTS

When choosing a franchise, remember:

- It should be a business that fits you financially;
- It should be something that fits your skillset;
- It should be available right where you live, so you're not doing excessive windshield time.

With those points in mind, let's close this chapter with a sampling of franchises in a myriad of categories. Please note: This is by no means a complete list, but rather a very small sampling to stimulate your thinking. Some of these companies I work with and some I don't. For more comprehensive lists, I urge you to visit the sites mentioned at the beginning of this chapter.

SERVICE FRANCHISES

Handyman
Mr. Handyman
Handyman Matters

Disaster Restoration
SERVPRO
ServiceMaster
AdvantaClean

Senior Care
Homewatch Caregivers
Comfort Keepers
Care Patrol
Right At Home

Painting Services
CertaPro
WOW 1 Day Painting
Pro Tect Painting

Cleaning
The Cleaning Authority
Maid Brigade
Molly Maid

Window Cleaning
Fish Window
Window Genie

Moving

You Move Me

College Hunks Moving Junk

On-site Repair & Restoration

Fibrenew

Creative Colors International

Lawn Maintenance

Lawn Doctor

U.S. Lawns

Coupons

Money Mailer

* * *

RETAIL FRANCHISES

Batteries

Batteries Plus Bulbs

Battery Giant

Signs

Speed Pro Imaging

Image 360

Specialty Retail

UPS Store

Post Net

Pizza

Papa John's

Little Caesar's

Domino's

Papa Murphy's

Pizza Hut

Restaurants

California Fresh

Denny's

Fuddruckers

TGI Friday's

Hotels & Motels

Holiday Inn

Days Inn

Motel 6

Automotive

Meineke

Midas

Maaco

Jiffy Lube

Hair Salons

Supercuts

Great Clips

Sport Clips

Massage

Hand and Stone

APPLY, VALIDATE, NEGOTIATE

Although this chapter is titled "Apply, Validate, Negotiate," I have divided it into four steps:

- Introduction
- Qualification
- Validation
- Negotiation

STEP 1: INTRODUCTION

It's time for you to meet the franchisor. This occurs with your intro call. Franchisors all have different ways of getting you information. It could be a series of one-on one-calls, live and pre-recorded webinars, or live and pre-recorded conference calls. Throughout the entire information exchange process you need to be cognizant that you're being evaluated on your business acumen, your behavior and that you actually do what you say you're going to do.

On that initial call, the franchisor will present an overview of the company and will most likely ask you a bunch of questions about yourself, including:

- How long have you been out of work?
- What did you do?
- How long did you do it?
- Does your spouse work?
- How many kids do you have?
- Do you want to stay in the area?
- Have you looked at franchises before?
- Which ones did you look at?
- What did you like?
- What didn't you like?

After that intro call, the expectation moving forward is that there will be a weekly call as long as there's mutual interest between both parties. On each call, they'll unveil more information, giving you a little bit of homework to do that will ultimately lead up to getting the FDD. There may be three or four calls before that happens, or the franchisor might send you the FDD after the first conversation.

They'll send you the FDD. You'll read it. There will be a Q&A period on the FDD with the franchisor. They may run you through a personality profile test. Most franchisors, if you ask, will send out a pro forma, a blank spreadsheet with your revenue streams running across the top and your expense accounts in a column running down the left side.

The next level after that is putting your business plan together.

We'll talk about that in the next chapter, "Final Steps." But in general, vetting out several companies will take 60 to 90 days or so. If you're not working and can dedicate full time to this, it goes much quicker. If you're working a full time job, it can take much longer. It just depends on how many brands you're looking at. If you're looking at one, you've got one-third the work versus looking at three.

STEP 2: QUALIFICATION

As part of the qualification process, the franchisor will ask you to fill out a form requesting your financial information. Sometimes they won't and will just go with what I already forwarded them.

An example: Before you get into validation, they give you an FDD and may ask you to do a market analysis of competition in your marketplace. Let's say it's a painting company. A franchisor might say, "Do you think you'd have time to get that all done by the end of next week or do you need a little bit more time?" So you set up an appointment with them to do an FDD review.

You or your spouse would come up with a fictitious painting job, and you would put out calls and emails to different local businesses to see what the competitive landscape looks like.

Caution: If the review time comes and you haven't even opened up the document, that's a bad signal that you're sending to the franchisor. Many have online tools to see if you even opened up the information. Your level of seriousness will be very evident.

During this qualification process, you should be on your best behavior and try to genuinely impress them. How would you impress them? Be on time. If you are running late or have a conflict, pick up the phone or email your contact and move the appointment back or cancel it.

I've been the guy on the other end of the phone, calling candidates, and I've seen all sorts of behavior that might tend to disqualify a person: arrogant people, people that don't listen, people that draw improper conclusions from data, etc. I've had people say to me, "This business won't work here. We already have a competitor in this market." That is an invalid statement. Any business that you look at, there's going to be competition. The goal is take market share away from the independents. Remember, you have a tremendous advantage over them. You're not going to be the only game in town. The question is can you be the best game in town?

Again, a reminder: You are being evaluated on your actions. In the eyes of the franchisor, the business acumen you display during the qualification process and pre-training is going to be the same business acumen you are going to bring to the business.

Here's something else that you should be aware of: Occasionally, you are in competition with other candidates for the same territory. Will you be competing against other people who are after the same area franchise? As a consultant, I will always ask that question of the franchisor.

Recently, I had a client who was looking at multiple concepts. Finally, he focused on just one. The franchisor ran him through the personality profile test, and he hit it out of the park. We found out from the franchisor pretty early on that they were working with someone else that was looking at the same territory. I said to my client, "Somebody else is looking at the turf. You need to pick up the pace if you want to catch up to him." Determined, he swung into action and completely overtook his competitor. He put himself in the A position.

I've seen instances in which a territory has been available for 30 years, and it all came down to whose signed contracts arrived in the franchisor's home office first.

STEP 3: VALIDATION

Before moving forward, it is absolutely crucial to speak to other franchisees and learn from them. Ask the franchisor rep for some email addresses and phone numbers of folks in business at different stages of development. Don't forget to ask for that "password" we discussed earlier so these folks know you're the real deal. Here are some questions that you should be asking:

- How long have you been a franchisee?
- What did you do before this?
- How did you find out about this franchise?
- What other franchise companies did you look at, if any?

- What intrigued you about this one? What was unique?
- If you had to do this over again, tell me a couple of things you'd do differently.
- If you had a choice to do this over again, would you go with this industry? If the answer to that is yes, would you go with this company?
- What advice would you give to a prospective franchisee?
- How would you rate your offsite training?
- How would you rate the ongoing marketing and support?
- How would you rate the company's proprietary software?
- How would you rate their infrastructure and office staff?
- Do you talk to your operations person on a regular basis and do you get value from those conversations?
- What have your greatest challenges been? Were these challenges a surprise and has the franchisor been helpful in assisting you work through those challenges?
- Could you share with me how long it took you to be cash positive?
- Could you share with me some of your yearly revenue numbers and what kind of net profit is left for you?
- I'm trying to fill in some numbers on a pro-forma and was hoping I could go down the chart of expenses so I can plug in some realistic numbers. Could you help me?

The answers to questions such as these will help you truly understand what the culture of that company is; you'll be hearing it right from the people's mouths that are in the trenches, doing this day in and day out.

The easiest way to gather this information is by emailing franchisees to set up talk times. If you want to talk with 10 franchisees, send out 15–16 emails to different franchisees. You might need to reach out to franchisees several times before they respond to you. Remember, they have nothing to gain by talking to you. Try to keep your calls on point and 30 minutes long. Some people will be Chatty Cathy's and others will be very reserved.

One more point: When you do your validations, make your initial phone calls outside of your immediate area. Why? In many situations, you will be perceived as a threat to the local franchisees. I see this happen all the time. I used to do this as a franchisee. That local franchisee might have accounts in the area you are looking at. With a protected territory franchise, that franchisee would have to give those accounts up once you open. That local franchise might have been looking to annex a second territory or a friend or relative might have interest.

STEP 4: NEGOTIATION

It's important to know which pieces of your agreement are worth trying to negotiate and which aren't. As we discussed earlier, there's no negotiating the first territory fee. It's a number that's published in the FDD.

There is another case in which you might be called upon to negotiate: a resale or when you purchase an existing franchise directly from the owner. There are good reasons why people sell: death, grave personal illness, divorce and retirement. In the instance of a resale, the distinct advantage is—if you're a qualified buyer and you sign a nondisclosure form—you're most likely going to have access to the seller's current year's profit-and-loss statement as well as their previous tax records. This is information that you're not going to get all filled in for you when you're looking at a new franchise.

If the seller won't show you those numbers right away, something's not right. They're either running two sets of books or getting paid cash and not running it through the system.

When you enter the process of a resale, what fees do you pay? There will be a price associated with the business. You'll pay for the phone number, good will, improvements and inventory. You will not pay another franchise fee. The price of the business is usually very negotiable, just like buying a house.

As an example, let's look at my Postal Instant Press franchise that I put up for sale in 1995. I worked out the financial arrangements with the other party. The franchisor then approved them and gave me the go-ahead. Then, the only detail that remained was what's called a transfer fee. That item will be listed in the FDD. I've always found transfer fees to be very negotiable. I've seen them in the $7,000 to $8,000 range, occasionally as high as $16,000.

As the purchaser, the transfer fee gives you the same training and support that the previous owner got when he was a newbie. You'll go to offsite training; the franchisor wants to give you every shot at learning the business.

So while negotiation is very limited when buying a new franchise, when you're involved in a resale, you have more latitude.

FINAL STEPS

You've done your research. You've spoken to someone at the franchisor's headquarters. You've talked to existing franchisees. At last, the finish line is in sight. Reaching it requires two elements: time and focus.

WHAT'S THE PLAN?

The next step is to put together a business plan. Although it might seem to be a complex and time-consuming task, there are numerous resources that will make your job easier.

For example, www.score.org offers a free, downloadable business plan template, helpful advice, and mentoring from business professionals who are often retired executives donating their time. It's the leading nonprofit organization in this category and it gets support from the U.S. Small Business Administration. A word of caution: Sometimes you'll be hooked up with a volunteer who is clueless about franchising; these are usually people from the public sector who have never run their own business.

Another valuable resource is your local Small Business Development Center. In addition to help with your business plan, SBDCs offer a variety of useful services geared for new businesses like yours. You will find a comprehensive, state-by-state list of SBDCs at www.sba.gov.

Or most franchisors will send you a blank pro forma with all the expense accounts in place. I'd say 90 percent of the franchise companies I work with will send this out. Some franchisors send it out automatically. Others you will have to ask. An example:

BUSINESS PLAN TABLE OF CONTENTS
From Score.org

I. *Table of Contents*
II. *Executive Summary*
III. *General Company Description*
IV. *Products and Services*
V. *Marketing Plan*
VI. *Operational Plan*
VII. *Management and Organization*
VIII. *Personal Financial Statement*
IX. *Startup Expenses and Capitalization*
X. *Financial Plan*
XI. *Appendices*

Once you've drafted your business plan, I suggest that you contact several franchisees including those you've spoken to earlier in the vetting process and ask them to look at your document. These are people in the exact same business that you're trying to join. Use them as a resource.

Later, when you've become an official franchisee, the franchisor will sit down with you and help you refine the plan.

TIME FOR DISCOVERY DAY

About 85 percent of franchisors require that you meet them in person before giving you final approval. Most of these companies will have one or two "discovery days" a month and, most times, multiple candidates will attend. Most spouses end up coming along too. FYI, attendance is by invitation only.

At the headquarters during discovery day, you will typically meet the entire home team. Each of them will come in, tell you about what they do and give you the most finite information they can about the company. They may accompany you to a couple of company locations. You'll talk to the IT guy, the marketing guy, the ops guys, a couple of the VPs and the CEO. Most times, you'll be flying in the night before since a typical discovery day will take up an entire day. Sometimes they'll take you out to dinner the night before or the night after. It's a good time to look everybody in the eye, shake people's hands and get a really good feeling (or not-so-good feeling) about the organization you're getting ready to join or not join. It's like a marriage contract...with a timeline.

Sometimes you'll be taking this trip on your own dime, but some franchisors will reimburse you for airfare. Some will only reimburse you if you come on board. Some will pick up the hotel room. They'll usually feed you. As a franchise consultant, I ask those questions up front.

On discovery day, the most important thing to look out for is a culture of being helpful. How friendly are the people you meet? What does their infrastructure look like? Who are these other people you're going to be working with? You're going to get a feel for things. Ever walk into a place and you just get the heebie-jeebies from it? You can't wait to get out of there! Then you walk into someplace else, and it feels good and warm. That's what it should feel like at the discovery day.

These people will be everything to you. They will be your mentors. They will provide guidance and life support for your business. It's crucial that you are comfortable relying on them.

GET APPROVED!

Meanwhile, back at the franchisor's headquarters after you leave discovery day, everybody that met with you will gather and talk about whether they think you'd become a good franchisee or not. They actually vote on you and they'll usually let you know within 48 hours. FYI, the voting, generally speaking, is a democracy. It's not like blackballing at a fraternity or sorority where it only takes one naysayer to nix you. Among my clients over the last couple of years, I've never had anyone be turned down because I've done a thorough job prepping them for the day. But, overall, people do get turned down.

Let's say a guy comes in from the West Coast; he's working with a New Jersey franchisor and he shows up at the discovery day in a t-shirt, shorts and sandals. Everybody else is wearing a sport coat and tie. Think they're going to take him? Nope.

At the very least, I'll brief clients on what to wear. Often, we'll ask for an itinerary ahead of time so I can help prepare them for the day. I will always schedule a prep call with you before you go.

There are a number of reasons why people get turned down. Are you respectful of your wife or are you a jerk? Face it: If you're not respectful of your wife, are you going to be respectful of your employees or your customers?

Often you'll be sitting down to a meal with a franchisor representative; you can find out a lot about somebody by going out to eat with them. Are you rude to the waiter? Did you order the most expensive items on the menu since you're not paying for the check? Did you get a little too tipsy at the bar that night and become rude, loud or boisterous?

It's safe to say that from the time you're in the company of the franchisor until the time you leave, you're pretty much under a microscope. Understand, too, that the franchisor is under *your* microscope. Are these people sincere and do they care about you? You should meet everybody that you're personally going to be working with. You probably don't want to work with 23-year-olds straight out of college who know nothing about the business, who are being trained as they go. You're going to want to have that senior ops guy in your corner.

Keep your eyes and ears open. It tells you a lot about a company if the operations guy has been there 11 years, another ops guy has been there nine years and the secretary has been there eight years. If that's the case, it's probably a pretty good place to work.

Once again, where does this positive atmosphere start? Usually with the CEO. He or she sets the tempo for the rest of the employees.

Not every franchisor conducts the discovery process the same way. There are many permutations. I have a franchisor I work with in Denver, a senior care company. They put candidates through a series of webinars. They make four presentations before they get the FDD to you. They'll set you up on a Skype call with some of the officers in the company before they bring you out for discovery day.

Meineke has a vetting process in which you talk to a couple of the senior level VPs and the marketing people. They've all got to give you a thumbs up before anything happens.

Today, you're seeing more and more of this type of interaction. You may have a one-on-one call with the president of the company before you come out to discovery day. It may be one of the VPs. Everybody is taking a pretty good look at everybody. As I often say, just because you have a pulse and a checkbook doesn't mean they need to take you.

Sometimes young franchisor representatives will try to get people out to discovery days too quickly in the process. I usually try to slow people down. It's preferable that you've done all of your vetting calls with the franchisor. You've gone through the federal disclosure document. You've put your business plan together. You've made all your validation calls and you have drilled down the territory with headquarters. All of that's been done before discovery. Just about everyone who attends a discovery day knows in their heart by the time the airplane lands back home if this is something they can do, can make money doing and have some fun with.

If you're still sitting on the fence two or three days later and think that you need more information, it's time to walk away. After discovery day, a client might say to me, "Look, I need to talk to more franchisees." No, you don't. Just walk away.

Last, and certainly not least, now that you're approved, it's time to sign the agreement. Of course, if you've done your due diligence, you've thoroughly reviewed this agreement because it's embedded in the FDD that you received earlier in the process.

So, here you are at the finish line. Now what?

It's show time!

PART THREE

SHOWTIME

———

GET PREPARED

The steps for the actual launching of your business fall into three categories:

- Meeting with your franchise attorney
- Pre-training
- Training

While, so far, you've been more or less on your own—researching franchises, digging up information, getting your financing together—the steps we'll discuss now are carefully choreographed.

ATTENDING TO LEGAL MATTERS

A franchise attorney is probably going to need to get involved before any contract is signed. This is a must, especially if it's your first time going through the franchising process. Keep in mind that this is another commitment on your part of financial resources and time.

Usually I'll connect my clients with a couple of franchise attorney referrals. I'm cognizant of the costs that you can incur sitting down with a lawyer and I don't want you to rack up a $3,000 bill for a clarity session. The price tag can be a little outrageous. Please remember most companies will not change anything in the contract.

After your meeting with the lawyer, it's time to sign your documents and send in your cashier's check or your wire transfer. Show time!

Show time always starts with the pre-training checklist, the business acumen checklist, the Right Start Program or whatever your franchisor calls it. All of these companies have a series of tasks that you need to accomplish before you arrive for training.

PRE-TRAINING STEPS

As an example of a pre-training list, let's take a look at a service business. In this scenario, the franchisor requires you to have an outside location; so, you've got to get that secured. You need to turn in your business information to the franchisor—address, phone numbers, etc.— so you can have all your printed material taken care of. They're going to give you an email address, and you'll need to get that synched up. Most franchisors will give you a web page, too. You need to get your insurance policies taken care of. You need to get your banking accounts set up. These are tasks that need to be finished before you go to training.

Typically, this is the time when I slow people down. Often, the following scenario occurs in December. The franchisor will say, "I realize you only have two weeks to get all this done, but our last training is Dec. 8th and we're not going to have another one until the third week of January."

I'll always tell my clients, "Let's wait until the third week of January. Let's make sure you've got your vehicle and it's got a logo on it. We need to make sure you've got all your pre-training done."

What happens is, when you haven't completed your pre-training checklist and you head off for training, you're gone for a week, two weeks, maybe even three weeks. You're having a hard time just handling the volume of information that's coming at you. Then you've got to return home, backtrack and take care of all the remedial stuff that you should have done beforehand. You should be going out, launching the business and trying to get your cash register ringing.

I've seen people fail to get the checklist done, or do it in a haphazard manner, thinking they're going to get the cash flowing more quickly by going to training sooner than later.

The list of pre-training tasks will depend on the brand you've chosen. Any time a retail location is involved, for example, it becomes a lot more complicated and takes a whole lot longer to accomplish. Think back to when you purchased your first house: it's complex in the same kind of way.

Most pre-training programs take two to eight weeks to finish everything up. Here are some examples of what you'll need to do:

- Establish banking accounts;
- Buying or leasing a new or very good used vehicle, then getting the vehicle wrapped;
- Getting incorporated;
- Getting your FEIN number;
- Setting up your DBA;
- Getting your marketing program in place to launch when you get back from your off-site training;
- Securing a location or outside office;
- Getting your insurances in place.

Every company will have a different pre-training list, and you will need to accomplish the tasks in a specific order. There will usually be a follow-up call with somebody at corporate headquarters every week or as you need help. Also, you'll have training manuals/videos to guide you along the way.

TIME FOR TRAINING

As you're going through pre-training, you will receive your off-site training schedule; you'll be going to the franchisor's corporate headquarters for up to three weeks, depending on what they have to teach you. Some franchisors may have you in for a week, let you go home for several weeks and bring you back in for another week. Why would they do this? They feel that there is so much information to process, that you might need a break. Some franchise companies may have you spend several days to a week shadowing a veteran franchisee after your off-site at HQ is completed and before you open.

As an example of what you might expect during training, let's look at a service franchise, specifically a residential maid cleaning business. First and foremost, they'll show you how to hire people, what to be looking for in a potential employee and how to conduct background checks. They'll teach you how to answer the phone, how to handle setting estimate appointments over the phone, how to go out to a customer location and do an estimate. During training, there's a lot of role-playing that goes on. They tell you what kind of supplies you should use, what kind of tech equipment you should use and what kind of vacuums you should buy. You'll learn where you should be advertising and how you should be tracking your advertising.

And even though they don't want the owner doing it, they will also teach you how to physically clean a place: how to clean a bathroom, how to clean hardwood floors, etc. This material is also in the training manual, and most companies have backup videos (in English and Spanish) to go with it.

In short, the franchisor is giving you everything you need, from marketing and financial guidelines, to execute the actual job that your employees will have to do. For example, if it's McDonald's, they'll show you how to cook a burger at Hamburger U.

Speaking of McDonald's, founder Ray Kroc is an inspiring model of an individual who knew by heart all aspects of the franchisee's job. He was known to actually scrape gum off the concrete sidewalk; I witnessed that myself at the Des Plaines store as a small child. And he himself actually put the franchisees through training on how to clean a bathroom.

This is a great example of a dedicated, cross-trained individual. He needed that Des Plaines location to be the paradigm of a McDonald store in order to promote and sell his franchises. And he wasn't above playing the role of cleaning man.

Use him as an inspiration as you go through your franchisee training.

RUNNING THE SHOW

Before we move forward into a discussion of running your business from day-to-day, I want to reiterate two important points.

In the lead up to your off-site training—in the weeks before—I urge you to take your time. Don't rush off to training until you've got all your pre-training boxes checked off. Complete those tasks, and not only will you enjoy a well-deserved sense of satisfaction, but you'll also be better able to focus on learning without the distractions of talking to your insurance agent, your real estate person, the guy getting the car for you, the contractor building out your facility, etc. All those boxes should be checked off in advance. You need to focus on learning.

THE BIGGEST MISTAKE

This book isn't going to get into the details of how to run your business. There are a thousand variables, and in almost all cases, the franchisor does a better job explaining them than I possibly could. This brings us to the biggest mistake a new franchisee makes when he opens his or her doors: He doesn't talk to the franchisor enough.

The franchisor is unquestionably the expert in your business. And even though you might think you're smarter than them, you'd do well to listen to their advice. Especially when you've joined a franchise that has an established system, there probably isn't anything you're going to run across that somebody else hasn't had to deal with.

So put your ego aside, along with your out-of-box thinking. When you need help, pick up the phone and call headquarters. These companies have processes and systems in place with the sole purpose of helping your business. So stop over-analyzing and just ask them for help.

Who do you ask? The franchisor usually assigns an operations person to you. That individual will be responsible for a given number of stores; the franchisor may break up franchises geographically by region. That person will make periodic field visits to your location. More on that topic soon.

Keep in mind that your operations person is being paid to be responsive to your needs. You'll have plentiful resources at the franchisor's corporate headquarters to help you through an accounting issue; to help get your Google Adwords program set up with the IT department; to assist with marketing materials such as e-brochures or ValPak ads. The list goes on and on. The moral of the story: You've got all these resources at your disposal; you just have to ask for help.

Many people like to question the established processes, the established systems. Let's be clear: The best new ideas do come from the field, but that's down the road. First, you need to get on the horse and ride it. The franchisor is going to tell you how long to ride it and where to park the thing when you get off. Once you've got the system figured out, you can bring your out-of-box thinking into play. If you don't master the system, you put yourself at a big disadvantage.

If you were vetting out some franchise companies and you came back to me and said, "Mark, I want to talk to some people that are doing mediocre and aren't making it," we'll find those people and I guarantee you one thing: These mediocre franchisees are not following the system. More specifically, in most cases they're probably not spending what they need to spend on marketing.

TURNING THE KEY
Franchise processes cover a lot of ground:

- How to hire people;
- How to do an estimate;
- Cleanliness standards;
- Proper forms to use;
- Proper vendors to use;
- Plus, anything you can think of from where to hang the mop, to where to stash the first-aid kit. The franchisor

tells you where everything goes. There's a method to their madness.

Here's an example drawn from my own experience with Postal Instant Press (PIP). My wife and I were off-site for two weeks of training. I did every single thing that was required of me before we got on that airplane to go to off-site training. While I was out of town, the PIP system kicked into high gear. Everything was delivered while we were gone.

When we returned, I put the key in the door and discovered that the place was ready to roll, right down to the smallest detail: the pencils were sharpened, the Scotch tape was in the dispenser, all the equipment was put together, all the inventory was unpacked. *That* is a sparkling example of a turnkey system.

Another big mistake that inexperienced franchisees make: They think they need to be everything to everybody and they start slashing prices, throwing their profits out the window. The franchisor's model was not built on price slashing. While it's true that all some customers care about is price, others care about quality, professionalism and being on time, and they're willing to pay your non-discounted prices to get that.

FIELD VISITS

When your operations person pays you a visit, there are a number of helpful tasks that they perform. They may do competitive price checks in your marketplace. They may combine that field visit with an audit, so an auditor comes in and examines your books, making sure that you're in compliance with everything that you're supposed to be in compliance with.

At a PIP location back in the day, for example, they had a checklist of 200 items, including the outside sign, windows clean, coffee area clean, copy area clean, etc. Everything that you're supposed to be doing is listed on a check-off form.

A field visit may consist of your operations person taking you by the hand and saying, "We need to start marketing the business. We're going to spend all afternoon marketing, so get all your stuff together and I'm taking you out on sales calls."

I am going to share a personal story with you that happened to me in September of 1987. We were set to have our 90-day follow up visit from PIP corporate. I was informed that, of everyone from that June training class, we were last in volume of the 10 new franchisees that were at that training class. I called corporate and asked if they could send out a marketing person instead of the operations person. They agreed.

A gentleman by the name of Ben Fretti arrived. Ben spent two full days with us watching production, how we answered the phone, did estimates and our overall customer service levels. At the end of day two, we locked up at 6:00 p.m. and Ben and I sat back in the production area. I will NEVER forget this. I was told we had a great location and our service levels were exceptional. Ben looked at me and said, "I need you to do three things to be very successful. It's up to you if you are actually going to do them or you can give me lip service that you will do them." Ben, who was not a big guy, brought his fist down on the countertop and hit it so hard, it created a hairline crack in the counter.

"Number one: You need someone out marketing the business 15 hours a week. If you're not going to do it, hire someone that will." I hired that person the following week, and for the next nine years, we had someone marketing the business 15 hours a week.

"Number two: Stop lowering your prices! You are not going to get every estimate you do. People will pay for professionalism, quality and on-time service." I stopped discounting except for high volume orders. Ben was right.

"Number three: Get involved in your community. You need to be networking." I got involved in four different service organizations and we got business because people knew us and trusted us, not because we had the lowest price in town. Thank you Ben Fretti for your sage advice almost 30 years ago!

FOLLOW THE PLAN

The most common place where people disagree with the franchisors is in their marketing plan. Bad idea.

Most franchisors will give you a dollar amount that you need to spend on a monthly basis. You'll have options on how to spend that money. Let's look at Window Genie, a franchise that offers customers window cleaning, window tinting and pressure washing. In the first year of business, they require franchisees to spend $48,000 in marketing. They have a contract with ValPak. They have an IT person who sets up pay-per-click services such as Google Adwords.

You need to spend the money, but franchisees don't always do it. For one reason or another, they fall short. You've got to spend A to make B, yet sometimes when they don't have enough cash, A ends up going to pay their mortgage because they went in undercapitalized. They didn't have their personal finances separated from their business finances.

You'll hear complaints such as "We ran a Money Mailer ad and we didn't get anything out of it. I just wasted $300." When you run ads, they are all very trackable. Perhaps the real problem was the front desk person who was on the phone with his girlfriend the whole day, or customer calls went to voicemail and nobody returned the calls. Or maybe the offer in the ad was subpar, like 10 percent off...At 10 percent, who cares?

People often don't realize that you must spend money to make money. I often tell a story about one of my neighboring franchise partners. Every single time we were doing a combo ad together, she pulled out on me the day the vendor needed to be paid. We did double to triple her volume.

Later she complained, "I don't understand why you're doing so much more business than I am..."

A residential house cleaning company such as The Cleaning Authority has it so buttoned down, they can tell you what your acquisition cost is going to be for a client, what the average time that client is going to be with you and the lifetime value of that contract. It's a very metric-driven business with a lot of historical data to go back on.

Some final key thoughts before we move on to the final chapter:

- Listen to your franchisor;
- Follow their marketing plan;
- Trust them;
- Take their advice!

CONCLUSION

Some people dream about becoming a physician or a police officer. Some people dream about becoming a teacher, a professional baseball player or an attorney. And many people dream their whole lives about starting a business. At first consideration, none of these endeavors would seem to have anything in common. Yet they do.

To succeed in these fields, you need dedication, stamina and diligence. If you have these qualities, stop dreaming; a franchise should not be something you fantasize about forever. If you have these qualities, do not be intimidated or held back by fear of the unknown, by the cost of getting into a franchise or by potential failure.

Starting any business is a lot harder than it might look, but there's good news: The franchise model makes starting your own business easier. It's one of the best ways for new business owners to succeed because, as we noted earlier, many of the systems and processes have already been figured out for you.

Also, you have someone to talk to on a regular basis if you have a problem. You have someone that will sit down and help you with budgets, marketing and a host of other important issues.

ON THE CUTTING EDGE

In addition, many franchisors pride themselves on their cutting-edge concepts, offering new ideas all the time like a new profit center, a new software package, a new phone application, etc. Gone are the days when a company like McDonald's offered a handful of products and resisted introducing new items to their menu. In this age of convenience and customization, when brick-and-mortar establishments are in constant competition with e-stores like Amazon, the ability to stay ahead of the curve is more important then ever. How forward thinking is the franchise that you're evaluating? It's one more factor to keep in mind.

THE RIGHT FIT

One of the reasons I've written this book is to hold the franchising process up to the light so you can examine at least some of the inner workings of this challenging yet immensely satisfying world.

Having said that—let me add a proviso: Getting into business isn't for everybody. Ask yourself what are you willing to give up to make it work? Many people aren't willing to give anything up. However, even if you're hard working and willing to sacrifice, even if the idea of opening a franchise appeals to you immensely, it just might not be the right fit for you. You would fall into this category if you have a rogue personality and you don't like to follow a system or play by the rules; if you don't have the necessary money to do it; if you don't have the necessary skillsets; if you don't have permission from your significant other to do it; or if you lack focus.

For example, I called a client six months after he opened the doors to his franchise. I knew, according to franchise guidelines, that he should be out doing 20 sales calls a day. What do I catch him doing on this particular morning? Redesigning the e-brochure, a serious deviation from his plan. To succeed, he needed new customers—he needed to be out doing his marketing.

TEST THE WATERS

Are you the type of person who likes to jump into a pool of cold water without dipping your toe in first? Well, get over it! The decision to open a franchised business should not be an impetuous one. Careful, clear-headed thinking is mandatory.

To illustrate the muddled thinking of a potential franchisee, here's the type of conversation with a client that I seek to avoid:

Client: "My friend Charlie is doing this business down in Albuquerque. He's knocking it out of the park."

Me: "Well, that's great. What's Charlie's background?"

Client: "He's a professional salesman."

Me: "And your background is what?"

Client: "I was a librarian."

Me: "Well...You may want to think this through a little bit."

Many franchisees fail, but it's usually because the proprietor chose the wrong franchise—which you can avoid by following the advice in this book—or because they didn't execute the plan that's been carefully crafted and tested by the franchisor.

Some franchisors have a post-training checklist, too. Some will actually have your first two months pretty well structured for you, with everything you need to be doing every day.

My advice: stick to your budget. Follow the roadmap. That's why you got involved in a franchise. Appreciate the value of the franchise that you are part of.

Occasionally I'll have a client say to me, "I don't see what I'm getting for all this money. I can do this on my own." I just sort of tilt my head back and say, "No, you can't. You'd have done it already. How are you going to compete with their website, with their e-brochures, with their proprietary software?" Every time I have somebody tell me they're going to try and go out on their own, they're gone in a year.

BEING A ROGUE

Earlier, I wrote that being a rogue was an undesirable characteristic in a franchise newbie. At the risk of contradicting myself, there is room for your out-of-the-box thinking once you've mastered the initial key concepts behind your franchise.

I've found most franchisors to be receptive to new ideas from someone who is successful and mastered the system. You usually need to ask permission with something new that you're doing and most times they'll say, "Go for it", unless it's immoral or illegal. In fact, franchisees generate some of the best ideas.

When I had my Postal Instant Press store, for example, we were doing a lot of fulfillment printing for NutriSweet, which involved shipping the finished pieces. It was working so well, we decided to add shipping as another profit center, competing with the local Mailboxes, Etc., by cutting their prices by 30 percent. It was an ancillary service for us, not our bread and butter. What a wonderful profit center that was!

As a franchisee, I was always looking for little extra things to add. I suggest that, once you're established, you do the same with the approval of your franchisor, of course.

HERE'S TO YOUR SUCCESS

Franchisors exist to make sure that their franchisees succeed. It's a simple matter of dollars and cents. Your success is of vital importance for them because the greater your success, the greater their profits.

If you've got the desire, the financial resources, the skills and the gumption, you can succeed, but there are two more necessary ingredients to add to your toolset: Trust in the franchise you've chosen and belief in yourself.

I know you can do this. You should know it as well.

HERE TO HELP

If you feel stuck or feel like you need more guidance in understanding your next step, consider using a consultant such as myself. There are approximately 3,000 franchise consultants in the U.S. However, the vast majority of them come from corporate life and have picked this livelihood as the next best thing. In my opinion, they lack the requisite experience.

Just as you need to do vetting as you enter into the process of trying to secure the right franchise, you should be using a similar process when looking for a consultant. When evaluating, I suggest that you look for a consultant that—in addition to business skills—has experience as a franchisee in at least one system, worked for a franchisor or has a long track record as a franchise coach.

That's part of what I bring to the table. I'll work to find the best franchise for you, get you set up with them and guide you through the whole process. There's no financial risk to you because my services are 100 percent free to you. It costs nothing other than your time.

Whatever your decision, I wish you the best of luck!

POSTSCRIPT

STEVE CIANO'S RECIPE FOR SUCCESS

Let's wrap things up by having a conversation with Steve Ciano, whose success story with Electronic Restoration Services started this book.

Mark: What made the ERS franchise model so attractive to you?

Steve: When I decided to explore franchising, I decided I was looking for a franchise that would have strong upside potential. I needed a company that would allow me to develop my own business by using their model, but not with overwhelming restrictions. Even though this franchise model was in its infancy and carried additional risk, I strongly believed the upside potential was worth it. Their oldest franchise was less then a year old. I was intrigued by the fact that there were many unknown variables (which still exist today), that there were and still are many unknowns, and that I would be getting in at the beginning and could help mold this company as it continued to develop. Although this business existed for over 20 years, the franchise concept to open across the country was less then two years old. The more due diligence I did, the better I grew to like the opportunity. The concept and basic business plan looked very positive, and I believed there was a much larger opportunity then I had seen in any of the other franchises I investigated.

Mark: To what do you attribute your great success?

Steve: My success (whether or not I would categorize it as "great") has come from using my past business experiences, following the basic business model that was presented and constant dedication to the plan. To quote a famous movie line, "Failure is not an option."

Mark: How much time to you spend in field sales, marketing and networking every week?

Steve: This is a tough question to give a direct answer to. In the beginning, I spent four days per week, 10 hours per day making cold calls. Then, after about three months, this went down to about three days a week on the road. Marketing is something I do at every opportunity presented to me. This can consist of a follow-up call, a cold call, an on-site visit, just a call to say hello, calling about a claim and selling expanded services, spending time explaining our services to the insured and making sure they are comfortable. These practices have been the cornerstone to increasing revenue.

Mark: Are you running ahead of your forecasted budgets for the year? Did you beat your forecasts last year?

Steve: Last year, we achieved 273 percent of the target that headquarters set for us. This year, they upped the target significantly based on last year's numbers. I expect to exceed it by about 25 percent. Through the first quarter, we've already invoiced 40 percent of our target and have another 25 percent in process.

Mark: How many of your family members are involved in the business?

Steve: My older son Joseph has joined me in this venture; he is a 20 percent owner and is my operations manager. My wife works about 25 hours per week helping with the bookkeeping and my 17-year-old son works when he can.

Mark: What advice would you give an aspiring entrepreneur looking at franchising for the first time?

Steve: Understand who you are and what your own capabilities and limits are, and make sure they match the opportunity you are considering. Understand that starting your own business will be very challenging and you will go through many ups and downs. Make sure you have the full support of your family and make them aware that getting this started will require most of your available time. Look at the cost and the cash flow that will be required to maintain this business; you do not need the added stress of underfunding. If you wake up in the morning and have the desire and passion to succeed on your own, then maybe it is time to go for it!

You may contact Steve at Stephen.Ciano@gmail.com

ABOUT THE AUTHOR

Mark Laughlin is an author, franchise coach and entrepreneur, with close to 30 years experience on all three sides of franchising: franchisee, franchisor and franchise coach.

He started his career in retail management back in the 1970s where he developed a reputation for being a turnaround specialist, before he developed the itch to run his own business and made the move into franchising.

Mark had great successes as a franchisee with three different franchise chains in three different niches—*Pip Printing*, *Molly Maid*, and *Inches-A-Weigh*—building each one to top performance levels before selling them for a profit. He then took his experience and expertise to the other side of the table and began working in sales development and coaching for a number of franchises.

In 2012 he moved to *The YOU Network* in 2012 in order to share his vast experience with others who were also seeking to better manage their destinies through successful business ownership.

Made in the USA
Middletown, DE
27 February 2019